HOWARD ROSS, a Chartered Accountant, is a Partner of Touche, Ross, Bailey & Smart, Canada, and of P. S. Ross & Partners, Management Consultants. A former President of the Canadian Institute of Chartered Accountants and a Chairman of the Institute's Committee on Accounting and Auditing Research, Mr. Ross has long had an active interest in the subject of his book. He may even be said to have acquired his interest at birth, being a third-generation accountant who continues a family professional tradition that dates back to the start of his grandfather's practice in 1858.

Much honored throughout his distinguished career, Mr. Ross is Chancellor of McGill University and an Officer of the Order of the British Empire and has received honorary degrees from Queens, Sir George Williams, and Sherbrooke universities. He did his undergraduate work at McGill and received an M.A. from Oxford, honoring in Philosophy, Politics, and Economics.

THE ELUSIVE ART OF ACCOUNTING

A Brash Commentary on Financial Statements

HOWARD ROSS, C.A.
PARTNER, TOUCHE, ROSS, BAILEY & SMART, CANADA

THE RONALD PRESS COMPANY • NEW YORK

Library of Congress Catalog Card Number: 66-16218

PRINTED IN THE UNITED STATES OF AMERICA

To my dear wife Dorothy

A balance sheet is a statement of the financial condition of the enterprise.*

A balance sheet does not purport to reflect and could not usefully reflect the value of the enterprise.†

These are old fond paradoxes to make fools laugh i' the alehouse.‡

* AICPA, *CPA Handbook*. † Committee on Terminology of the AICPA. ‡ W. Shakespeare.

Preface

It is no part of an accountant's job to be gullible. He is by training a professional skeptic. Thus no accountant would dream of setting out on a dissertation on financial statements without confessing that he personally took a devastatingly critical view of the current state of the accounting art. But there are doubts and doubts, and I would like to make it clear at the outset that I am somewhat proud of the sweeping and all-embracing scope of my own doubts. In fact the only time I have encountered anything equal to them in intensity was when reading of the religious doubts of Mr. Prendergast, the delightful little unfrocked clergyman who appears in Evelyn Waugh's classic novel *Decline and Fall*.

To show what sweeping doubts Mr. Prendergast and I are capable of, let us start with his story as Evelyn Waugh tells it:

> ". . . If things had happened a little differently I should be a rector with my own house and bathroom. I might even have been a rural dean, only"—and Mr. Prendergast dropped his voice to a whisper—"only I had *Doubts*.
>
> . . . .
>
> "Ten years ago I was a clergyman of the Church of England. I had just been presented to a living in Worthing. It was such an attractive church, not old, but *very* beautifully decorated, six candles on the altar, Reservation in the Lady Chapel, and an excellent heating apparatus which burned coke in a little shed by the sacristy

door; no graveyard, just a hedge of golden privet between the church and the rectory.

"As soon as I moved in my mother came to keep house for me. She bought some chintz, out of her own money, for the drawing-room curtains. She used to be 'at home' once a week to the ladies of the congregation. One of them, the dentist's wife, gave me a set of the *Encyclopædia Britannica* for my study. It was all very pleasant until my *Doubts* began."

"Were they as bad as all that?" asked Paul.

"They were insuperable," said Mr. Prendergast; "that is why I am here now. But I expect I am boring you?"

"No, do go on. That's to say, unless you find it painful to think about."

"I think about it all the time. It happened like this, quite suddenly. We had been there about three months, and my mother had made great friends with some people called Bundle—rather a curious name. I think he was an insurance agent until he retired. Mrs. Bundle used very kindly to ask us in to supper on Sundays after Evensong. They were pleasant informal gatherings, and I used quite to look forward to them. I can see them now as they sat there on this particular evening; there was my mother and Mr. and Mrs. Bundle, and their son, rather a spotty boy, I remember, who used to go in to Brighton College by train every day, and Mrs. Bundle's mother, a Mrs. Crump, rather deaf, but a very good Churchwoman, and Mrs. Abel—that was the name of the dentist's wife who gave me the *Encyclopædia Britannica*—and old Major Ending, the people's warden. I had preached two sermons that day besides taking the children's Bible class in the afternoon, and I had rather dropped out of the conversation. They were all talking away quite happily about the preparations that were being made on the pier for the summer season, when suddenly, for no reason at all, my *Doubts* began." He paused, and Paul felt constrained to offer some expression of sympathy.

"What a terrible thing!" he said.

"Yes, I've not known an hour's real happiness since. You see, it wasn't the ordinary sort of Doubt about Cain's wife or the Old Testament miracles or the consecration of Archbishop Parker. I'd been taught how to explain all those while I was at college. No, it was something deeper than all that. *I couldn't understand why God had made the world at all.* There was my mother and the Bundles and Mrs. Crump talking away quite unconcernedly while I sat there wrestling with this sudden assault of doubt. You see how fundamental that is. Once granted the first step, I can see that everything else follows—Tower of Babel, Babylonian captivity, Incarnation, Church, bishops, incense, everything—but what I couldn't see, and what I can't see now, is, *why* did it all begin?

"I asked my bishop; he didn't know. He said that he didn't think the point really arose as far as my practical duties as a parish priest were concerned. I discussed it with my mother. At first she was inclined to regard it as a passing phase. But it didn't pass, so finally she agreed with me that the only honourable thing to do was to resign my living; she never really recovered from the shock, poor old lady. It was a great blow after she had bought the chintz and got so friendly with the Bundles." *

In the realm of accounting, what bothers me is not that there are three different methods (all fully sanctioned) of handling bond discount, nor that there is chaos in certain particularly difficult areas such as accounting for oil exploration, nor even that there is some question whether the very principles on which financial statements are based can ever be set down in detail in a manner that will be completely acceptable to all authorities.

Like Mr. Prendergast I am worried about something much more basic. The fact is that I am confused and in doubt as to the purpose of the whole system of financial reporting on which so much ingenuity and hard thinking have been lavished. *Precisely what are we supposed to be accomplishing by issuing financial statements?*

Once granted that there is a defensible and explicable purpose in financial reporting, I can see that everything else follows—deferred tax accruals, standard costs, depreciation of fixed assets, negative goodwill, capitalization of lease-

* (London: Chapman & Hall, Ltd., 1928.)

purchase contracts, and all the rest of it. Once over the main hurdle, these present no special difficulty—any more than the Babylonian captivity, incense, or the consecration of Archbishop Parker did for Mr. Prendergast.

This book attempts to establish what financial statements should accomplish in contrast to what they actually do accomplish, to explore some of the reasons for the apparent shortcomings, and to point out a road towards improvement.

The ideas that have woven themselves into this text have been collected and matured through the multitudinous contacts that occur over a long professional life. Teachers, authors, clients, competitors, and above all, the professional associates with whom one has worked—all contribute inspiration and criticism. It would be quite impossible to unravel all these influences and to prepare a rational list of those who have contributed to any value that this dissertation may contain. In any event, it may very well be that some of those who might be named would not particularly appreciate finding themselves associated with some of the conclusions reached. The fact that no formal acknowledgements are made does not mean there are none I would wish to thank, but rather that there are too many—not that I have no feelings of indebtedness, but that I am overwhelmed with them.

HOWARD ROSS

Montreal
January, 1966

Contents

THE ELUSIVE ART OF ACCOUNTING

A Brash Commentary on Financial Statements

1

The Present Scene

PERHAPS OUR ACCOUNTANTS should envy our space-research scientists, who have had the enormous stimulation of being faced with headline after headline announcing that a Russian in outer space has just accomplished another feat hitherto considered by our scientists as beyond our present competence. It is a pity no Russian accountant has come up with a satisfactory type of financial statement to shake the monumental complacency of our accounting establishment.

We badly need a cool examination of the state of our financial reporting, and reference here to outer-space research is not too far-fetched. Basically the same fundamental necessity should be driving us towards improvement in both fields. The importance of scientific research in this age of headlong and lethal competition can presumably be taken for granted. The importance of financial reporting should be almost equally apparent, as such reporting is, in the battle for survival, a basic element in the system of communication used in all planning and decision making and in measurement of progress. In short, proper financial reporting is essential in efficient industrial production and indeed in almost any form of organized human activity.

Case for the defence

Quite a good case could be made for the present state and past progress of our financial reporting. Undoubtedly such reporting has achieved a certain status. No modern corporation would dream of issuing securities without a prospectus containing up-to-date financial information in conventional form. We can review past scandals and reflect comfortably that they could not happen now—or at any rate not happen so easily—owing to current standards of disclosure. Undoubtedly statements are getting better.

As the years go by, published statements become more informative—for example, by disclosure of additional key information, such as total sales (long regarded by corporations as a profoundly important management secret). There has also been the gradual acceptance of the notion that indiscriminate use of secret reserves can make misleading nonsense of a set of statements.

Looking back over past developments, the accounting profession might perhaps be tempted to be complacent. Accountants have achieved a genuine professional stature in what must surely be record time. The first professional body of accountants was organized just over a hundred years ago —which is just yesterday as the lives of professions are measured. Yet in many countries today the profession has established standards that get top recognition at least in the difficult and important areas of integrity and reliability.

Before giving the accountant's art the sort of critical going-over that is the prime purpose of this book, it might be well to emphasize what a remarkable achievement it is to have developed a type of financial statement that gets reasonably general acceptance—even if such acceptance is qualified and taken with some reservation by the knowledgeable.

The fact is that the operations of the larger modern corporations are almost unbelievably complicated. A corporation often manufactures a wide variety of products requiring raw materials from various parts of the world. Its finished products may be subject to changes in fashion, competition from newly invented materials, and other hazards of progress. It is likely to deal across international boundaries—introducing the complications of tariffs, foreign exchanges, and unfamiliar tax systems. In view of these complexities and enormous size, it is something of a miracle that, a few weeks after the end of a fiscal year, a set of financial statements can be published that summarizes down this mass of varied and complicated activity to a couple of dozen figures—and that this can be done so skilfully, with such good judgment and such recognized integrity that the resulting statements are taken seriously by those who need, for one reason or another, to appraise the progress of the corporation. The published financial statements of a corporation are indeed taken most seriously—and there are those who are content to look only at the final summary of the summary that appears in the financial pages of our newspapers as the increase or decrease in earnings per share. It would be interesting to know how many of those whose hearts leap up at the announcement of an increase in earnings per share have any idea of the estimates, judgments, and conventions that must go into all such calculations.

A great deal has been said in praise of the ingenuity of certain species of ants who apparently carry on a crude form of agriculture and have learned to separate out battle groups of their stronger members and teach them to form fours and march. It might be only fair to pause briefly in admiration of human beings who can organize and carry on the infinitely complex operations of modern business. Financial statements are of course an essential part of this process.

Current criticisms

However admirable the development of financial reporting has been, it has nothing like kept up with the growing need for better statements. A certain amount of criticism is of course necessary and good, but even the best financial statements published today are subject to truly devastating criticisms—and it is disturbing that most of the criticisms come from the more thoughtful and knowledgeable observers.

A great variety of groups are interested in financial reporting and each group tends to have a somewhat distinctive point of view. Consequently criticisms come from many different angles. They may nevertheless be sorted out into two general categories—the criticisms that come from those who are concerned with financial statements because they need to use statements in their work, and the criticisms of those who are interested in financial statements because they have the responsibility of preparing them. The users and producers have quite different problems to worry about and their criticisms must be considered separately.

Statement users

The users are a mixed lot but they, again, may be divided into two main groups—the insiders and the outsiders. The inside group consists of the managers who require financial statements to make decisions in running a business. The problems of the managers are highly specialized and it is coming to be recognized that management accounting is a quite distinct subject. While there are serious problems in this area, and it is an area of overwhelming importance, it is best regarded as a subject for special study quite distinct from the general system of financial reporting that is the main concern of this book.

This general system of reporting is designed to satisfy the needs of a variety of outsiders—such as the shareholder who wants to follow the progress of his business, the prospective investor who wants to know whether to invest, the banker or supplier interested in credit risks, the tax assessor, the economist studying the progress of the economy, and so on.

However much difference there may be in the detailed requirements of the outsiders, they all have the same two basic demands: statements must be reliable and they must be informative.

On the grounds of reliability, those who use statements have little to complain about. For the last hundred years at least, the whole attention of the accounting profession and of government regulatory bodies has been concentrated on the prevention of fraudulent or misleading statements. This important battle has been in a fair measure won. However, in the process, the second and more important of the two basic requirements of those who use statements—that they should be informative—has been largely neglected.

The chief criticism of contemporary financial reporting by statement users is simply that the statements do not give them the information they seek.

In general terms, what is required is a statement from which the current financial strength and progress of an undertaking can be judged. What is actually provided is a type of statement that appears to give just this sort of information but that in fact does not do so. What financial statements describe as "net income" (to take an important example) is not really net income in the sense in which anyone but an accountant would understand the term. For one thing, the accountant's "net income" is a figure arrived at after the systematic writing-off (or amortization) of expenditures made long ago that have absolutely no current relevance to anyone but an accountant. Moreover the financial strength of the enterprise is set forth by listing its assets in a mixture of current and conventional values which results in a quite meaningless total.

Asking for a fish and receiving a serpent

It is no wonder then that, in spite of the admirable progress there has been in financial reporting, there are very serious criticisms heard from the most responsible and reflective quarters.

As *The Economist* thunders:

> Anyone who knows anything at all about accounts knows that at almost every turn—the value of stock, equipment and buildings; the method of accounting for research, development and publicity expenditure; the apportioning of tax—the book entries depend on judgments which may possess a large element of guesswork and certainly could have been, equally legitimately, expressed by a different method with totally different figures at the end.
>
> Many accountants will say that this is largely unavoidable, and that what really matters is that a consistent code of procedure should be applied in each case. The better firms of accountants long ago ceased to conform to the old image of arguing over the last halfpenny shown on the petty cash whilst assessing stocks by little more than rule of thumb and a handful of old bills. But they may

still fall into much more dangerous complacency towards the realities of economic change. The profession has been notoriously slow to admit the effects of inflation on the value of capital assets. . . .

All this means is that an accountant, trained in a narrow and often spurious exactitude, can easily fail to recognize the distinction between, first, a historical record of stewardship, and, second, a clear statement of the current standing of a company in wealth and profitability and in comparison with previous periods—and other companies.[1]

Equally sweeping criticisms from unquestioned authorities could be easily found; and this should not surprise us because accountants in their most solemn pronouncements have made it quite clear that the financial statements they prepare do not even purport to provide information about solvency and profitability. For instance, anyone might be pardoned for thinking that a conventional balance sheet is prepared to show the financial strength of a company by listing its obligations against its resources and to establish its net value. But this is not at all how a balance sheet is defined in accounting texts. Here is a fairly typical definition of the balance sheet:

A tabular statement or summary of balances (debit and credit) carried forward after an actual or constructive closing of books of account kept according to principles of accounting.[2]

The situation would be serious enough if it were simply that those for whom financial statements are prepared are not getting from them the information they want; but the situation is potentially even more dangerous than this. The

[1] November 21, 1964.

[2] Committee on Terminology of the American Institute of Certified Public Accountants as quoted in Norman J. Lenhart, C.P.A., and Philip L. Defliese, C.P.A., *Montgomery's Auditing* (8th ed.; New York: The Ronald Press Co., 1957), p. 100.

fact is that, in spite of the most devastating criticisms of the concepts of income and value on which conventional statements are based, such statements are nevertheless seriously studied by investors, analysts, creditors, and others; and every day literally millions of important decisions are being based on the earnings reported in such statements. This is presumably because there are simply no other figures for an investor to go on.

Surely someone should shed a tear for the investor who buys shares in a company because one of the credit balances "carried forward after an actual or constructive closing" of its accounts exceeds the credit balance in that account carried forward after the actual or constructive closing of the previous year. Or for the investor who concludes that a business has changed from a profitable to an unprofitable operation merely because the balance appropriately carried forward in the net income account is a credit one year and a debit the next. Yet this is apparently what any investor is doing who attempts to draw any conclusions whatever from increases or decreases in the reported net income of a company.

One of the most admired investment ratios is undoubtedly return on capital employed—calculated as a percentage of net income to investment. Yet a contributor to an English accounting journal, signing himself "Unrepentant Heretic," has this quite fair comment to make:

> Given time to reflect on the doubtful validity of our accounting conventions, it would seem that, having made nonsense of profits and nonsense of capital employed, we deduce by expressing one nonsense as a percentage of the other, a return on capital employed, by which we may compare the performance of one company's index of nonsense with that of another.[3]

[3] *The Accountant* (The Institute of Chartered Accountants in England and Wales), November 14, 1964.

The custodians of the accounting art

So much (for the time being) for the problems of those who use statements. A quite different point of view can be detected in the accountants whose interest in statements stems largely from the fact that they have the responsibility of producing them.

It should be mentioned, by way of clarification, that the accounting profession divides itself into two parts. In the first place, there are the professional accountants employed by corporations to operate their systems of financial reporting and control and, in the second place, there are the professional accountants in "public practice" whose essential function is to give an independent professional opinion on the reliability of a corporation's published statements. It should be evident that these two parts of the profession have somewhat different roles. They have both, of course, an interest in the general development of the art, but the actual statements of a corporation are essentially the responsibility of the management of the corporation, which includes the professional accountants in its employ. The independent professional man in public practice who audits the accounts has simply the responsibility of reaching an opinion on whether or not the statements prepared by the corporation present a fair picture.

While in actual operation the inside and outside accountants work closely together in the production of a set of statements, it is clearly understood between them that the prime responsibility lies on the accountants who form part of the management team.

While it is natural that those who use statements should want as much information as they can get, it is equally natural that those charged with the heavy responsibility of producing statements should hand out information as cautiously as possible—this is the basic reason for the difference in the points of view of the users and the producers.

It has been already emphasized that the problems of producing a modern statement are almost impossibly difficult; and all the accountant's prejudices are, quite predictably, in the direction of confining statements to the demonstrable recorded facts of actual receipts and expenditures, with only the most reluctant ventures into the chancy fields of estimate, valuation, and judgment. To produce any statement, a fairly large element of estimation and judgment just has to be used—but the pull of the accountant always tends to be away from the subjective and towards the objective. His attitude is likely to be something like this: "I know you would like to have all asset values brought up-to-date, but this would involve appraisal, a notoriously uncertain process, and it would probably be safer if we stuck to the actual supportable values at which the assets were purchased for hard cash—even though the purchase took place many years ago. After all, we can avoid the possibility of anyone being misled by the irrelevance of these values if we explain quite clearly that this is the basis on which the statements have been prepared."

Unfortunately the situation is complicated by the fact that the users and producers of statements tend to be mutually exclusive groups. Those who use statements are probably only infrequently skilled in statement production; whereas accountants tend to lose interest in a statement once they have succeeded in producing it. This makes for a sort of mutual lack of sympathy with each other's problems between users and accountants.

To summarize: The final result is that conventional statements tend inevitably to be a compromise between what the user would like to have and what the accountant is prepared to take responsibility for issuing. While it is easy to sympathize with the accountant's position in this tug-of-war, it should be fairly evident that better statements will never be produced unless accountants accept the fact that they must be much more venturesome. They must produce something closer to what users want rather than what the accountant thinks they should want or at least what he thinks they should be satisfied with.

In deciding on what form of presentation is best, the starting point and prime concern must always be the needs of the statement user. No statement can be defended unless it tells someone as clearly as possible something he ought to know in order to help him do something he ought to do. This is not a dazzling new insight. In a pamphlet issued as long ago as 1934 by the American Institute of Certified Public Accountants we read:

> The aim should be to satisfy (so far as is possible and prudent) the investor's need for knowledge, rather than the accountant's sense of form and respect for tradition.[4]

Concepts of income

As there has been no proper reconciliation between what the accountant is prepared to vouch for and what his readers wish to know, the notion has developed that there are legitimately several different concepts of income—the accountant's concept, the investor's concept, the economist's concept, and so on. There are indeed these differing concepts —but not legitimately. There should be only one concept of income and the varied points of view of all concerned

[4] *Audits of Corporate Accounts.*

should be reconciled—not simply accepted as natural and understandable.

What everyone who asks about the income of a business really wants to know is the amount by which the value of the business has increased. This concept of income as increase in value must be accepted. It should of course be conceded that inevitable limitations are encountered when attempting to measure the value of a business corporation—including the absolutely unbeatable problem posed by the fact that many valuable attributes of a business are simply not measurable. But if the accountant cannot be expected to produce the perfect income statement by measuring the unmeasurable, surely he can be expected to measure increase in measurable values as well as they can possibly be measured. In other words, his concept of income must be increase in value too, with only the qualifications that are absolutely essential to make owing to the inherent impossibility of measuring all values perfectly. The fact that he cannot achieve perfection should not alter the nature of his view of income.

Interpretation of financial data

It is important to dispose of one apparent method of dealing with the problems of divergent concepts that is really quite illogical. This is the notion that the accountant should confine himself to compiling financial data in a systematic manner satisfactory to himself, leaving the "interpretation" of his figures to economists or investors or others. The accountant is thus supposed to deal only with the factual, leaving those who use the statements to do their own interpreting. This is what must happen to a certain extent. Each analyst is likely to make his own calculations and adjustments; but the accountant must always, through both his professional skill and his detailed knowledge of the accounts, be in the best position of anyone to apply judgment and make the basic interpretations necessary to produce useful statements.

We must get rid of the idea that there is something wrong in an accountant using his head. As our friend Unrepentant Heretic has put it:

> Knowing the limitations of conventional reporting, being in possession of far more information than is ever likely to become a statutory obligation, does the industrial accountant best serve the interests of his company by leaving the interpretation of "the state of the business and future potentialities" to someone looking in through the shop window? It seems very anomalous that the professional auditor should confine himself to reporting on so-called historical facts, which can only be true or fair on the basis of specified conventions, but which, except in the light of these conventions, may be reasonably fair but seldom true. By contrast, the financial analyst, who may well be a member of the same profession, is primarily concerned with his views thereon despite the limitations placed on his scope by the absence of much essential data known or available to his professional brother.[5]

The necessity to reconcile the accountant's point of view and that of the user cannot be so easily side-stepped. If say the economist fails to find in the accountant's statements the information he wants, he is forced to make supplementary calculations of his own—often making in the process adjustments that seem amateurish and ill-conceived to the accountant. The only satisfactory solution is for the accountant to accept the challenge of producing statements that come as close as possible to meeting the economist's requirements. The apparently conflicting views of the accountant and economist will only then be reconciled in the best feasible compromise.

[5] *The Accountant,* November 14, 1964.

It will be argued later that all statement users, despite apparent diversity, need the same basic information, and what has just been said of economists applies to investors, creditors, and others as well.

The important point for the accountant to remember is that he must stop pretending there is any merit in a conception of income, however logically developed, that no one is interested in.

The accountant's self-doubts

There is a great deal of healthy arguing and self-doubting amongst accountants themselves. Skepticism is something they tend to be good at, and the debates in their journals are often tinged with an encouraging (because it indicates they care) acrimony. But the perfectly extraordinary fact is that practically none of this good wholesome disputation centres around the one basic important question that confronts the profession—namely that the best of financial statements are not only failing to do their job but are apparently not even designed to attempt to do such job.

The literature of accounting is, naturally enough, full of pronouncements that emphasize the importance of statements in guiding investors, bankers, and others—but equally full of pronouncements that insist that anyone would be wrong to assume that statements purport to set forth values in the generally accepted sense of the word and that, in fact, they can really only be understood by the professionals who prepare them and know the rules.

Moreover these quite irreconcilable views are sometimes solemnly expressed by the same authority without explanation, embarrassment, or "any mitigation or remorse of voice." What is badly needed is someone to cry: "You simply cannot have it both ways. You cannot pretend your statements are worth studying and also avoid responsibility for them by disclaiming any intention of preparing them on the only basis they could possibly be useful to anyone."

If accountants fail to come to grips with this bedrock issue, what (it might be asked) do they spend their time debating? The very considerable amount of time they spend in theorizing is consumed in yelping contentedly down the familiar trails left by a variety of red herrings dragged across the scene long ago.

Several of these false trails will be explored later in this book. For the moment we might consider, by way of illustration, the hottest debate that has raged recently in accounting circles. This is the question of the extent to which accounting rules should be uniform and authoritative as opposed to judgmental and flexible. Here is an important and difficult problem well worth discussing. This is one of those pleasant topics for debate on which a great deal of good sense can be talked on both sides. Clearly uniformity is a desirable quality in statements as it makes important comparisons much more significant. On the other hand flexibility has great merit, as too rigid a uniformity can produce quite unacceptable results in the infinite complexity and variety of the business world.

There is nothing wrong with exploring and discussing this kind of problem. Some of the relationships encountered are subtle and intriguing. It might be possible to develop certain Parkinsonian laws such as: The degree of authority with which a pronouncement is made varies indirectly with the extent to which such pronouncement is specific.

However, no matter how important this question is, it should be obvious that it is almost completely a side issue until we reach a clearer consensus on what financial statements really should purport to show.

Business in the jet age

One of the complicating factors in discussions of financial reporting, which is often overlooked, is that business is now carried on in an environment of almost breathless change. This change pervades everything and profoundly complicates the problems of accounting. For instance in the perplexing field of generally accepted accounting principles, it is sometimes implied that our troubles would be over if we could only produce a listing of such principles that aroused what the AICPA describes as "substantial authoritative support." But this is not the case. The changes and particularly the speeding up of new developments in the business world are constantly creating new problems and thus creating new requirements for information. In a parallel way, new inventions in the data processing field are introducing startling new possibilities in statement production. Hence the basic point of compromise, insisted upon above, between what the statement user wants and what the accountant feels he can conscientiously produce, is constantly shifting. Thus even if a completely satisfactory listing of accepted principles could be produced, it would immediately start to be outdated by new developments on both the demand and supply sides of the communicating business. It might perhaps be argued whether a detailed listing of principles would be useful; but, beyond all argument, what is much more essential is the development of a technique through which generally accepted principles can be kept up-to-date. The pursuit of better financial reporting is of course an unending one. No matter how much progress we make, we will always need further improvements.

The important point to remember is that no matter how rapid the continuing changes in financial statements may be, such statements must always remain a compromise between what is wanted and what can be produced at a given point in time.

Theory and practice

The development of financial statements has essentially been by trial and error. Statements have been evolved by observing the best current practice and innovations, and imitating them. At certain key points in accounting history the courts, or, more recently, regulatory commissions, have made pronouncements; or new statutory provisions have been introduced—but such court decisions and new legislation have simply followed and codified developing practice.

Consequently a priori reasoning plays relatively a small part in accounting. It is largely a common sense art developed to provide useful information for practical business men. In the pursuit of consistency (early recognized as a vital factor) and to systematize its procedures, certain rules were evolved that might be dignified with the description "accounting theory." But theoretical reasoning weighs lightly in accounting; and a crusade to improve accounting theory cannot be justified unless it leads to the actual production of more useful financial statements.

There has been much good talk, many ingenious rationalizations of the accountant's position, and some stimulating intellectual exercises, but not nearly enough progress in producing better statements.

Accounting doctrine—a mixed bag

It will be argued, a little later on, that to try to develop accounting theory into a profoundly philosophical study is simply a waste of time. It is not this kind of subject. Accounting is a practical, common sense discipline. However this does not mean that clear thinking is not required. We do indeed require the coolest, most clearheaded survey of our dogma.

Accounting doctrine consists of a miscellany of propositions that the accounting profession has come to adhere to over the years. It is rather a mixed bag—including the obviously profound and the profoundly obvious. There have been many efforts at reform, but these have tended to get off on the wrong foot. Sometimes the reformers have started out with the assumption that this is a deep and difficult subject. As some of our beliefs are clearly basic and important while others are procedural and less weighty, there have been efforts to set up an elaborate philosophical system by dividing our small store of accepted maxims into categories—such as postulates, principles, procedures, conventions, and what-not—each with its own degree of profundity and sanctity. This may have value as an intellectual exercise but it has little relevance to the task of producing better statements.

We must recognize that our so-called generally accepted accounting principles are simply ways of producing financial statements, which have, over the years, gained a measure of support.

These "principles" need to be considered carefully. Some of them have little validity and should be discarded forthwith. Others are profoundly useful and should be cherished. It will in fact be found that to some of the basically valid principles, the accounting profession pays little more than lip service. Much better financial statements would be produced if accountants clasped these sound precepts to their hearts and followed out their full implications. Of these, perhaps the utility concept is the most overwhelmingly important.

Donnybrook Fair

The battle for better financial reporting should not be a private scrap amongst accountants; it is everyone's fight. One of the troubles with past efforts to reach satisfactory principles has been that accountants usually tackle the problem by themselves rather than in active collaboration with those whose needs are supposed to be served.

One of the most discouraging aspects to this whole subject is the general inclination of business men to dismiss serious discussion of statements with, "Of course I am no accountant." The implication is that it is not up to them to have any opinions in these matters and yet they are the very persons for whom the statements are ostensibly prepared. If they cannot understand them, what use is it preparing them?

It was Walter Bagehot or someone who is said to have expired with the classic death-bed pronouncement that "We must learn to look at things more from the point of view of the consumer." However unlikely this may be as a historical accuracy, it certainly makes pretty good sense as an admonition—in the present case, at any rate, it is completely applicable. Statements must be looked at from the point of view of end use rather than from the technical production angle.

Plan of attack

The whole discussion of financial reporting will be a complete waste of time unless the following propositions are fully accepted from the start:

1. The best of our statements are unsatisfactory and we must do something to produce better ones.
2. Techniques of statement preparation must be developed that will make it possible to meet more fully the needs of statement users.
3. It is essential to reach agreement on a general concept of income that will be acceptable to the generality of statement users and producers. This can only mean acceptance of the idea that income means basically increase in value.
4. The foregoing concept of income means that assets must be stated at current values or the closest possible approximation thereto.
5. Accounting dogma requires a complete overhauling and accountants must stop subscribing to totally irreconcilable views.
6. Our accounting system must be appropriate to a rapidly changing world. It is not sufficient to develop merely a reporting system that is the best available under today's conditions.

To establish these propositions beyond argument and to explore their full implications, it is necessary to work systematically through a chain of argument that starts by explaining how we got where we are, and leads through to a suggested program for dealing with our difficulties.

In the succeeding chapters of this book we will first review, from the start, the function of financial statements in the business world, and the emergence of the conventional balance sheet and income statements as basic documents. It will then be argued that usefulness is the sole criterion by which statements can be properly judged, and that in attempting to develop the most useful statements we can only make progress by recognizing that accounting is a species of language and must be so regarded. Its rules are pragmatic and do not constitute a profoundly philosophical revelation of eternal verity. It will be necessary too to examine in detail some of the wrong-headed convictions that have plagued us and some of the special problems of management accounting and the determination of taxable income.

The stage will then be set to present a program for improving our reporting to keep up with the rapidly changing economic world in which we live.

2

The Conventional Balance Sheet and Income Statement

WHILE THERE IS, quite literally, an infinite variety to the types of financial statements that may be produced, the whole of accounting theory has centered around the development of one particular type: the balance sheet and related income statement of a commercial enterprise. As a necessary preliminary to tidying up our accounting thinking, it is desirable to consider the fairly elementary question of how these statements came to acquire their unique importance, and why they create the basic problem with which both accounting profession and business world have struggled so long, namely, the establishment of a code of generally accepted accounting principles. Were it not for the special problems raised by commercial balance sheets, certainly we would have developed very different principles—if, indeed, we had felt obliged to develop any at all.

Almost any record of money transactions intended to provide data on which someone will base a decision can be described as a financial statement. As the decisions that need to be made in business vary all the way from relatively casual decisions (such as which customer a salesman will call on next) to decisions of categorical importance (such as whether a new plant will be built), it follows that all sorts of presentations are appropriate to meet requirements in different circumstances.

While there are interesting problems in all fields of accounting, the main concern of this book is with commercial statements, where the really difficult problems are encountered. However some observations on non-commercial accounting are included in Chapter 6.

The business world

In the business world we run into a kaleidoscopic variety of organizations—all the way from the man selling pencils on the street corner to the largest of international complexes. However, whatever the size and whether carried on as an individual operating by himself, as a partnership, or as an incorporated body, in all cases carrying on business is essentially a process of making decisions—of all kinds: large and small decisions, long-term and current decisions, carefully considered and snap decisions.

Decision making in business may be either quite casual or highly formalized, depending on the size of the business and also on the idiosyncrasies of the business man. However, whether the operation is casual or highly organized, the business process is essentially one of planning and then checking progress against plans.

The purpose of financial statements is to help provide a basis on which decisions can be made as intelligently as possible. The aim is to narrow down the essential elements of guess-work and risk that are present in most business situations.

In very small businesses (such as our man selling pencils) decisions can be made easily, directly, almost without reflection. The operator in such cases is like the bush pilot who flies his airplane "by the seat of his pants." However, operating a business on even a slightly larger scale than this requires the collection and analysis of financial information for the two processes essential in business—making plans and checking progress against plans.

The general idea in financial reporting is to give two pictures: firstly a picture of the current position to show what resources are available and what obligations the business is committed to; secondly a picture of recent operations from which past success and future prospects can be judged, and plans can be made.

Developing needs

The bewildering complexity of modern businesses has developed over the past couple of hundred years from simple, small-scale beginnings. Increasingly sophisticated financial statements have been developed to meet the needs of larger enterprises and faster tempos.

From the point of view of financial reporting, perhaps the most important development of all has been the tendency for ownership and management to separate as businesses become larger. In a small enterprise, run by the owner, there is clearly a need for only one type of general statement. There are many small businesses operating today for which this is still the case. However in our large public corporations, ownership and management have become entirely divorced. There are thus two groups to consider with quite different requirements, and it has become evident that one type of reporting cannot satisfactorily meet the needs of both. Simple and self-evident as this may seem today, the idea that accounting for management and accounting for owners are two distinct problems, calling for quite different techniques, dawned on the business and accounting world slowly, uncertainly, and cloudily—and not before much time had been wasted and confusion generated. For years managers were told that they should rely in running their business on guidance provided by statements prepared largely on principles designed to protect creditors and investors. On the other hand, investors have sometimes been persuaded they should be satisfied with data prepared partly on assumptions that were designed for those responsible for management decisions.

In other words, the general assumption until relatively recently was that one type of accounting could satisfy the needs of both management and of such "outsiders" as shareholders or creditors. This was indeed generally the case a hundred years ago—but not today.

Self-evidently, management usually require more frequent and more detailed information than shareholders do, but this is not the crucial distinction that must be made. The reason that management accounting and what has come to be called custodial accounting differ in nature as well as degree is that the management team are insiders and everyone else is an outsider. Management are insiders because they not only use the statements but have the responsibility for producing them, whereas all others use the statements but are not in any way involved in preparing them.

The reason that this distinction is so decisive is that management have complete control over the accounting system that produces the statements. They not only know on what assumptions, procedures, and principles a statement has been prepared, but also control the selection of such assumptions, procedures, and principles. In short, management can suit themselves and can produce the information they want. What other companies are doing, or what others might desire if they were running the company, need not concern management; they have the responsibility for running the company and control over statement production and, as far as their own requirements are concerned, they may please themselves.

No other group is in this position. Shareholders, creditors, and others must take statements at their face value. This is, of course, not literally true. Important creditors can, in certain circumstances, get the right to make special investigations into what lies behind a statement. Shareholders may ask questions, and management, through the annual report and in other ways, give out a certain amount of background information, but the distinction between those on the inside and those looking in through the shop window remains valid and decisively important.

Management accounting

For a long time, the full implications of management's special position were not appreciated. This is not too surprising. The whole development of accounting theory is recent. In pioneering one must expect rough-hewing. It was only when statements had advanced to a certain stage of refinement that there was time to analyse differences in point of view. Be that as it may, we have now reached a point at which it becomes evident that we must stop trying to persuade insiders and outsiders that they must be satisfied with the same form of presentation. Otherwise, financial statements will remain, to a large extent, what they are today—an unhappy and unsatisfactory compromise between what is needed for two different purposes.

Management accounting is then best recognized as a special subject. It bristles with all sorts of fascinating difficulties and is of course of great importance, but it is not the main concern of this book. Some observations on management accounting are ventured in a later chapter, but this book concentrates mainly on the problems of published statements, the only statements with which the general theory of accounting is concerned. It is only in preparing such statements that we come to grips with the battle-torn problem of generally accepted accounting principles.

The variety of information requirements

Having narrowed down the topic of financial reporting by eliminating consideration of non-commercial enterprises and the specialized problems of management, we are still left with a wide variety of statement users. Amongst these are such groups as shareholders, prospective investors, bondholders, bankers, suppliers, tax collectors, government regulatory agencies, and many others who have reason to study a corporation's performance. Also there are economists and analysts of various sorts who need information about corporate operations in the course of studying general economic trends.

Each of these interested groups has a somewhat specialized point of view. Some are particularly concerned with short-term solvency and some more especially with long-term potential. Some are directly interested in earnings and some only indirectly as an indication of continuing solvency. Ideally a special form of presentation might be designed to suit the particular needs of each user, and in fact this is done to some extent in practice. A banker worried about a large overdraft may require a statement with very full details of receivables and inventories. A prospective investor considering a major investment may want past earnings analysed and presented in some special manner. In cases of threatened bankruptcy, a special type of statement prepared on a basis of liquidating values and priority of creditors may be needed. However, preparing special forms of statements is expensive and can be justified only if large sums are involved or some special urgency exists. It is thus fortunate that it has been found possible to develop general purpose statements that answer reasonably well the needs of most of the outside users, and that can in any event provide certain basic information which can be supplemented in cases of special needs.

The general purpose statements thus developed are the statements ostensibly prepared for presentation to the shareholders at the annual meeting. These statements, accompanied by an independent professional opinion from the company's auditors to the effect that the presentation is a fair one, have achieved an official status and are used not only by the shareholders, to whom they are addressed, but in the financial community generally.

General purpose statements

In accepting the possibility that general purpose statements can be usefully prepared, we take one of the decisive steps in accounting theory, a step making necessary the establishment of acceptable rules for preparing such statements. As important steps of this sort should be taken not casually but soberly and advisedly, we should pause at this point to challenge the concept of general purpose statements and to satisfy ourselves that there is indeed a sound basis on which they can be prepared.

It has been emphasized that different people approach financial statements for different reasons, and we should recognize one further hard fact: that there is an easily reached limit to the amount of information a statement can give without becoming hopelessly complex and confusing. Can, then, one set of statements satisfy so many different groups?

The answer the accounting profession has developed over years of discussion is: Yes. The reason that everyone can make do with one type of statement is that, however specialized their points of view, basically what all of them want to know is: Is the company in good shape? Thus they all want to know what the company's assets and liabilities are currently and, seeing that the strongest position can deteriorate rapidly if the company's operations are unsatisfactory, they also must know the trend of operations.

Given data on these basic points, the supplier can form some reasonable opinion of the risks he would take by selling to the company on credit, the shareholder can form some opinion on how management has fulfilled its stewardship responsibilities, the prospective investor can make an informed guess on the company's future, and so on.

Thus a type of general purpose statement has gained currency. Such statements must circulate, as it were, like negotiable documents, that is, on their face value. If they are to be read and interpreted intelligently, they must be prepared on some generally recognized and agreed basis, and anyone who has access to such statements must be able to rely on this assumption.

Perhaps it might be pointed out just once more that this is not a consideration that enters into the preparation of statements for management or for those who require special purpose statements tailored to suit their particular needs.

In this way general purpose statements have led us into developing, over the years, what are usually described as "generally accepted accounting principles." The word "principles" may have certain philosophic overtones, but in accounting the so-called principles are in point of fact simply sound and safe rules drawn from the best commercial practice.

From time to time some of these "principles" get embodied in statutes or confirmed by court decisions. They are dealt with in accounting texts and, more recently, have been elaborated on in the pronouncements of professional accounting bodies; but it is nevertheless fair to say that the generally accepted principles of accounting have never been fully and authoritatively codified to anyone's satisfaction. It is a thesis of this book that these principles never will be codified and that this does not matter.

While disturbingly different results can be produced by selecting one acceptable method rather than another that is equally acceptable, considering the size of the problem, it is perhaps fair to say that, by and large, a reasonable degree of comparability amongst the published statements of large corporations has been achieved. It must be admitted that there are exceptions to this—for example in the oil industry no satisfactory method of arriving at profits has been developed. This is not because uniformity is not desired, but rather because of the genuine technical difficulty of arriving at the best concept of profit in an industry subject to all the vagaries of searching for oil.

The balance sheet and income statement

The basic general purpose statements are of course the familiar balance sheet and income statement. These provide answers to the two big questions: How strong is the financial position of the company and is it making progress or not? To provide this information in an intelligible form, the statements have to be highly summarized.

One of the problems with the balance sheet and income account is that they show what the present position is and how the company got there; whereas what most people would like to know is: What is likely to happen to the company next? Some concession to this fact is made in preparing the income statement in that large non-recurring or extraneous items are segregated to enable the presentation of a more or less "normal" picture of operations, on which the investor may more safely base his projections of future developments.

It is of course a mistake to look for too much from a balance sheet and income statement. What these statements purport to give is a very simple, drastically summarized view of the resources and earning record of the corporation. We are often admonished that we must not try to add apples and oranges into one total and yet, in producing a balance sheet, that is exactly what one must do. Cash in bank, securities, deferred charges, inventories, buildings, machinery, and a variety of other types of property must be added together to get a figure for total assets. This is not the sort of problem that anyone in his right mind would want to tackle for the fun of it, but to produce an overall picture, it simply must be accomplished. It is also necessary to measure the value of assets whose value is virtually immeasurable. Goodwill and other elusive assets must somehow or other be dealt with.

It is here that some of the basic problems of accounting enter. How should the value of different kinds of property be established? Once this is agreed on, everything else follows reasonably simply.

The fundamental problem in financial reporting may then be stated as the problem of finding the most useful way of measuring asset values to produce balance sheets and income statements of as much significance as possible.

In the various types of special purpose statements, the accountant's task is to meet, to the best of his ability, the needs of the particular person or group for whom the statements are prepared; while in the contrasting case of general purpose statements, the object is to prepare statements that are in accordance with generally accepted principles.

Progress report

It is easy to see how the reassuring comments on our progress in financial reporting come to circulate. A tidy and beautifully systematic method has been devised for summarizing key information about business enterprises. Superficially at least (and most things tend to get judged superficially), there is general agreement on the form and content of financial reports, and the accepted forms seem to provide just the sort of general picture of conditions and progress that most people would want. The balance sheet sets forth assets in logical categories, showing separately those that are liquid and those that are more or less permanently committed. The income statement gives basic information on operations.

There is nevertheless a great deal of well-informed dissatisfaction with our financial reporting. That there are critics is not in itself a bad thing. In such a difficult field, probing self-criticisms will always have an important place. The really disturbing thing is that the accounting profession seems, at the moment, to be like an old windjammer slatting about in irons, unable to fill out its sails and set off on a decisive tack.

A leading journal of economic affairs should not be able to say (as *The Economist* did recently) that our financial statements are "stewardship accounts which are a necessary element in commercial probity, but have no constructive bearing on economic advancement." In an article headed "What is the Use of Accountants?" this journal goes on to observe:

> Accountants generally are still so far from recognizing the potential of their role as precision-tool makers for management that they seldom take the parallel step of advocating the release of more, and more realistic, information to shareholders. Though some accountants employed in big business complain, possibly rightly, that they are used as a cloak for the timidity of their board members, the truth is that if they really used their position to press for the release of franker statements—and for the new Companies Act that is overdue—they could have an enormous influence.

Discussing trends in both Britain and the United States, it adds:

> Conversely, if reform of the law does come about, the accountants and their clients and employers might find themselves being forced to think more clearly. It is significant that in America the accountants responsible for the public companies supervised by the Securities and Exchange Commission indulge in more ferocious argument and much more serious thought about the need to develop and define sensible accounting principles. It is fair to say, indeed,

that they have more to contend with—the inconsistencies of American company accounts are notoriously the despair of investors. But one does not need to agree with those who press for extensive standardization to believe that accountancy in Britain could become more efficient and its job more relevant if it scrapped the old textbooks and set out to define its aims and methods in twentieth century language. This may sound harsh to those familiar with the professional courses in new techniques, with the bulk of painstaking research and recommendations on matters ranging from the evaluation of stock-in-trade to tax reform organized by the Institute of Chartered Accountants, and with contributions of original thinkers from many branches of the profession. But this is no more than is expected, in their own fields, of doctors and engineers. To come back to the fundamental question, it is the accountant's field itself that needs defining—what he is best suited to do in the world today as well as how he can do it better.[1]

Observing these interesting developments from neutral and mid-way ground, Canadians can appreciate the enormous contribution the professions in Britain and the United States have made to the accounting art throughout the world, and can agree that the great task for all of us is to clarify our concepts and restate our position in today's language. The despair of the investors may be fractionally less intense in Britain, as *The Economist* seems to imply, and the arguments about accounting principles may be a bit more ferocious in the United States, but the situation is serious enough everywhere to require a thorough overhaul of our entire doctrine. One thing we conspicuously do not need at the moment is any more sounding of uncertain trumpets. We do not need a wild dashing about in all directions so much as a contemplative review, step by step, of the dogma we think we subscribe to.

[1] November 21, 1964.

3

Hard Facts, Mystic Rites, and Useful Statements

IF WE ARE to overhaul completely our accounting doctrine, we should start with fundamentals. We should attempt a clear statement of the basic objective in financial reporting.

At first sight this appears deceptively simple. If the purpose of financial reporting is to assess the current condition of a business and its past performance or future possibilities, this might seem, as explained in the preceding chapter, to be adequately provided for by a balance sheet that summarizes the present position and an income statement that sets forth past performance. But the real problem is: How can such statements be prepared to be as useful as possible? There persist two wrong-headed notions of our basic objective—one simple-minded and one highly sophisticated—that must be dealt with.

The truth, the whole truth, and nothing but the truth

The simple-minded error is to assume that our problem can be solved by stipulating that we should "stick to the facts" and prepare "true" statements. This glosses over a basic difficulty: that no one has ever found an answer to jesting Pilate's question, "What is truth?"

We can of course legitimately talk of true and false financial statements in the sense that some statements are prepared honestly and carefully while others may be produced fraudulently or carelessly. The former are reliable as far as they go and the latter are not. However, the important point for present purposes is that, even granting honesty and care, we are still left with the problem of what is a "true" picture. Apart from manipulation or careless errors, what sort of picture should the accountant be trying to produce?

In other disciplines, the concept of truth may well be appropriate. Philosophers search for ultimate reality. Theologians talk of eternal verities and scientists of the immutable laws of nature. In each case, there is the suggestion of some final and definitive standard against which all approximations may be measured. If this sort of thing works for the experts in these fields, more power to them, but in accounting it will not work at all. The line of reasoning and type of language that may be acceptable in philosophic or scientific fields have no relevance in statement preparation.

One authority puts it this way:

> Accounting has been created and developed to accomplish various desired objectives and, therefore, it is not based on fundamental laws or absolute precepts. Since accounting has evolved over many years through trial and error, it should be continually improved on

a basis that is responsive to the requirements of those groups in our society who use the end product—financial statements.[1]

It comes naturally to us perhaps to think of anything involving money transactions as solid and down-to-earth—just the place, one might suppose, for a straightforward factual presentation without philosophic elaborations. And you can say this for accountants, they have tried desperately to confine themselves to actual cash transactions, in the conviction that there is something meritorious and intrinsically valid about a transaction "backed up by hard cash." In fact, however, the subjective element in financial reporting is very much more pervasive than is generally supposed and, to anticipate a later conclusion, the only hope of progress lies in an increasing reliance on valuation—involving a still further retreat from objectivity.

As that extremely quotable expert "Unrepentant Heretic" puts it in summing up nearly forty years of experience:

> If there is one lesson one learns during an accounting lifetime it is that there is no absolute truth in figures. . . . It is time the accounting profession did something to eliminate the conglomeration of half-truths which we may have inherited but should not pass on to succeeding generations.[2]

Developing complexities

For the simplest business situation, it is indeed possible to suggest a form of presentation that is practically unchallengeable. If, for example, a man's only asset is $100 in

[1] George R. Catlett, C.P.A., "Factors That Influence Accounting Principles," *The Journal of Accountancy* (American Institute of Certified Public Accountants), October, 1960. Also found in W. J. Baxter and Sidney Davidson (eds.), *Studies in Accounting Theory* (London: Sweet & Maxwell, Ltd., Law Publishers, 1962).

[2] *The Accountant,* November 14, 1964.

cash and he has no liabilities, and if he spends his money buying goods he resells for $140 in cash, it would take some pretty slippery reasoning to devise an income statement for him in any other form than

Sales	$140
Less: Purchases	100
Profit	$ 40

Our accounting difficulties begin as soon as things get the least bit more complicated. Take for example the question of capital investment in "fixed" assets, defined by accountants as assets acquired to benefit more than one accounting period. If a delivery truck is bought for $2,000 and is expected to be in service for five years, it is easy to agree that the cost should be amortized or recovered over this five-year period. The whole problem arises in deciding how the cost should be spread so that a satisfactory profit may be calculated for each year. Consider some of the possibilities:

1. There is something to be said for the simplicity of charging $400 to each year—the so-called straight-line method of providing depreciation.
2. It can be argued that the truck will be likely to give better service when new, and that it would therefore be preferable to write off the cost by the diminishing balance method—by a fixed percentage of cost less accumulated depreciation to date.
3. There is also a method based on mileage rather than time, on the grounds that more cost should be charged against a year in which greater use is made of the truck.
4. Still another approach is to appraise the value of the truck at the end of each year and write off the amount by which the value has decreased.

These are just a few of a great many supportable methods that could be suggested for determining the annual cost of the truck. In fact, such is the variety of possible solutions, there is sometimes a tendency to select straight-line depreciation on the grounds that it is at least the simplest method. At times this tendency has been so strong that this method has come, through familiarity, to seem the natural or right method, and any other method is regarded as under- or over-providing depreciation.

The important thing to observe is that all these methods are conventional and arbitrary. Each method may have some degree of reasonableness and good sense, and the likelihood is that some may be better than others for certain types of fixed assets; but there is no one ultimately right way to establish the "true" amount of depreciation.

A rather special kind of situation is encountered in companies like railways or public utilities which own vast quantities of such assets as ties, rails, poles, and power lines. Where dealing with such large quantities, it is possible to make engineering studies of the life expectancy of these types of assets, and thus to determine what gets to be described as a "scientific" depreciation rate. But even here the best calculations can be upset by the quite unpredictable factor of obsolescence, and for any but these special cases an attempt to be scientific is quite farcical.

The same sort of vagaries are encountered in other areas. It is easy to allocate a cash sale to a specific period; but installment sales, in which collection extends over several periods, immediately introduce the problem of allocation, and thus an arbitrary rule of some sort. An even more difficult problem arises in long-term construction contracts. How much profit or loss has a contractor made when he has undertaken to put up a building for a specified price, and comes to the end of a year with only the excavations completed and the foundations partly poured?

The problem accountants face in weighing the conflicting attractions of authority and flexibility in their rules can now be seen for the horrifying dilemma it really is. If they attempt to maintain that one method only should be used, they must arbitrarily select a method from amongst several that are perhaps equally good. In this situation, it is difficult to expect the general agreement needed to sanction the method. Moreover, it is almost certain to turn out that in some circumstances another method than the one authorized can be demonstrated to be more suitable.

On the other hand, if this kind of strong line is not taken, and a variety of methods is sanctioned, a much more reasonable approach may be attained; it does result, however, in authorizing several different figures of profit, any one of which may be accepted as properly calculated. In this way we lose important advantages of comparability.

The intrusion of uncertainty

Faced with the choice of selecting arbitrarily one method from amongst several more or less equally good ones—and attempting to give this one method all the force of Holy Writ—or, alternatively, of conceding that there are several different accounting treatments that are equally acceptable, accountants have chosen diversity. This decision was probably inevitable. Whatever the problems of admitting a variety of proper results, it would surely be unthinkable to attempt to enforce a rigid acceptance of one method when such method could not be demonstrated to have any unique merit or validity. In this connection it should be remembered that the problem of diverse procedures applies not only to the fixed asset, instalment sale, and construction accounting mentioned above for purposes of illustration, but throughout almost every aspect of financial accounting.

Inevitable as the acceptance of diversity may have been, it has entailed the abandonment of any claim to absolute truth in statements. If several different profits are sanctioned, no one can claim any of them are "true." That accountants recognized this can be inferred from the gradual changes that were introduced into the wording used by auditors in giving their professional opinions on statements. The tendency at first was to allude to "the true and correct" position. This became softened to "a true view"; then to "presents fairly" the position. Finally we get to the current practice of qualifying the declaration by referring to fair presentation "in accordance with generally accepted accounting principles consistently applied."

It is easy to understand how auditors evolved the current wording. Nevertheless, an uncharitable critic might perhaps suggest that the subtle transformations in the wording of auditors' opinions were more likely to soothe the auditors' consciences than to alert their public to the actual state of affairs.

The significant conclusion, from all these developments, was that accountants had to abandon any notion of absolute truth for their statements, and to fall back on the claim that the statements were prepared in accordance with a system of rules, conventions, and principles whose logic and validity were demonstrated by the fact that they were "generally accepted." The great trouble with this solution was that when users of statements began to complain that financial statements, however systematically prepared, were not providing the basic information they required, the accounting profession tended to be driven into the position of claiming some intrinsic merit for their statements even if they did not provide what the statement users wanted. This was, then, the highly sophisticated position into which the profession gradually entrenched itself.

Here we begin to encounter the concept of a distinctively accountant's view of profit and value—a view largely ritualistic. Thus statements become not something to show the condition of a business, but rather something produced by the application of a set of esoteric rules known to the initiated. As one of the profession has put it:

> Hence we [accountants] are justified in continuing to use our accounting concept of depreciation on a historical base, applied consistently in our accounting and reporting, and allowing the economic concept full play in decision making with respect to pricing, dividend distribution, etc.[3]

The current situation is, then, that we have been led over the years (by a series of decisions, as so often happens, each one of which in itself appeared sensible enough) to the perfectly ridiculous position of defending accounting as some sort of good in itself—rather than as the handmaid of business.

It is important that we should reflect seriously on the full implications of this point of view, which runs through a great deal of accounting thinking. It is exemplified, for instance, in the discussion on historical costs in the authoritative *Accountants' Handbook*. We find these remarks in the section summarizing the case in favour of this method of valuation:

> Wilcox and Greer (Journal of Accountancy, vol. 90), commenting on the complexities involved in the use of revaluation data, say:

[3] L. A. Braddock, C.A. (Australia), in a paper delivered at the Third Conference of Asian and Pacific Accountants in Japan, 1963.

Accounts are kept, profits are computed, and policy decisions are made by several hundred thousand individual businessmen and their bookkeepers and clerks. Most of them would have grave difficulty in applying or even comprehending the principles of measuring cost expirations in terms of hypothetical purchasing power. The economic data available to them are certain to be inadequate and their interpretations of several dozen tables of price-index numbers are likely to be diverse to say the least.

They add:

The diverse uses to which financial statements are put call for basically consistent, understandable presentations, adaptable by intelligent but not clairvoyant readers to their own needs. Price-level adjustments do not lend themselves to such presentation.

Dohr (Journal of Accountancy, vol. 77) describes the case for historical cost data in plant asset valuation in these words:

In dealing with the fixed assets it is suggested that, on the whole, the cost basis is preferable in the light of the basic objectives of accounting. The function of the accountant, in recording and reporting the facts as to such assets, is primarily one of dealing with the cost of acquisition and the amortization of that cost over the useful life of the assets; the statement of assets at any balance-sheet date involves primarily a showing of the extent to which cost is unrecovered or unamortized and the extent to which the evidence indicates the residue is recoverable in the normal course of business. The accountant is not a valuer and he does not, for the most part, concern himself with present values; he is largely concerned with the business enterprise as a going concern. It follows that accounting is generally on a cost basis and that there is and should be a strong presumption in favor of statement in terms of cost.[4]

It is certainly a sobering thought that financial statements are being prepared by people who would have grave difficulty in comprehending "the principles of measuring cost expirations in terms of hypothetical purchasing power"—in other and simpler words, the ground rules for establishing the most reasonable current valuations. If they have difficulty grasping such essentials, it may well be wondered what

[4] Rufus Wixon, Ph.D., and Walter G. Kell, Ph.D., C.P.A. (eds.), *Accountants' Handbook* (4th ed.; New York: The Ronald Press Co., 1956), p. **18**.23.

they are doing issuing financial statements on which others are encouraged to rely. If this is indeed happening, no wonder readers must be "clairvoyant" to adapt to their needs the information provided.

Moreover, is the primary function of the accountant really to deal with "the cost of acquisition and the amortization of that cost over the useful life of the assets"? Is not the accountant's primary function better conceived of as the task of presenting those who need it with information that will be useful to them in making decisions? Not that he is a professional appraisal specialist, but should he not be able to comprehend the valuation processes sufficiently well to be able to work with such expert specialists in reaching the best available valuations? How else can he expect to undertake the responsibility of preparing statements that must involve working with cash equivalents of a variety of assets of different natures? Each asset must be taken into the statements in terms of cash. This is unavoidable; no statement could be prepared on any other basis. A valuation may involve a whole group of specialists in different areas; but surely those ultimately responsible for issuing statements must be able to understand these things at least to the extent, say, of being able to make a reasonable decision on which of several possible index numbers would be most appropriate in a given case.

This view of accounting as something divorced from the business and financial world would appear to relegate it to a sort of game for which the rules are made up quite independently of the usefulness of the results. A game is not utilitarian. It is an artificially set-up contest to bring out skill. For instance, in golf it makes perfectly good sense to have a rule that the club-head must not be grounded in a sand trap, but certainly no one would suggest that this is the best way of assuring that one will get a golf ball out of the trap with the fewest possible strokes. Similarly, the rules of football may provide great sport and entertainment, but they are not meant to present the best plan for getting a football from one end of a field to the other.

We must not let these red herrings, dragged across the trail so persistently, divert us from our basic function of providing useful information to those who need it.

Utility

It is no very earth-shaking conclusion that accounting is utilitarian—that a statement can be justified only by its usefulness. Most accountants would concede this readily enough. However, as may be seen from the quotations just given (and others throughout this book), this is not a concept accountants persistently adhere to in all its implications. They permit all sorts of inconsistencies to enter the picture.

There is even some tendency to cling to the absolute-truth concept. No self-respecting accountant could today profess formally to hold this view, but sometimes accountants talk as though they do hold it. You find them referring to some deviation from accepted practice as "distorting real profits" or "understating profits." Executives without accounting backgrounds are even more prone to this kind of thing. When we emerged from World War II into a period of inflation, for example, attention naturally was focused on the inadequacies of conventional depreciation practices. At that time annual reports were full of references to the resulting distortions in financial statements. It was customary to report that the statements "overstated" profits or that they did not "give the true amount of depreciation." What was actually meant was that the system of determining profits which had worked reasonably well (at any rate, acceptably) during periods of stability was no longer doing so under conditions of inflation.

This may seem somewhat of a quibble, but we will never get our thinking straight if we do not mind our language.

Different views of profit

We have been discussing thus far a general view of business operations. It is perhaps worth stressing that while such a general view is an essential in developing a useful system of reporting, terms like "profit" and "asset value" necessarily have different meanings in different contexts.

Profit can be calculated quite properly, in a variety of ways. Some of these are more appropriate than others for particular purposes. As a simple example, consider the question of whether interest on borrowed money should be deducted in arriving at profit. There is no absolute answer to this question. It depends on the use to which the resulting profit figure is to be put. For example, the board of directors, when deciding how much profit is available for distribution as dividends, must naturally take interest into consideration. On the other hand, an investment analyst comparing the profit-earning capacity of two firms would normally eliminate interest in order to compute the amount of profit the enterprises can generate. For such an investment analyst the question of interest comes later when considering financing.

Thus, while it is quite clear that to ignore interest expense when calculating a company's "earnings per share" would be an error of simply inconceivable grossness, when the profit-making capacity of a number of businesses is under study, the deduction of interest could be misleading.

Derivative principles

Utility is so completely fundamental in accounting that the validity of all other objectives rests on their usefulness.

Consider, for example, the important accounting virtue of consistency. Consistency is a good thing, but this is simply because statements prepared consistently from year to year are more useful than statements prepared on different bases. One of the popular tools of statement analysis is the use of comparative trends, and these can usefully be prepared only if the statements are consistent from year to year. Similarly, as has already been argued, uniformity of practices among companies is desirable as it makes comparisons more reliable and significant. This in turn, however, is because the inter-company comparisons are useful, and uniformity facilitates them. This can be further appreciated by the fact that such comparisons are really useful only when made between reasonably similar companies. The statements of a department store, for example, can usefully be compared with the statements of other department stores. There would be less value in comparing the statements of a department store with those of a public utility; and, consequently, while uniformity of procedures for all department stores might be strongly advocated, there would presumably be less enthusiasm for promoting uniformity between department stores and public utilities. In other words, uniformity is a good objective where it is useful—and not where it is not.

The corollary of materiality

Another corollary of the utility concept is the important one of materiality. A great deal of effort is wasted in the preparation of financial statements in analysing, refining, and sorting out items that have no appreciable effect on the picture. The result is often to clutter up statements with irrelevant detail, whereas what is wanted is a clear-cut picture of a few simple but important aspects of the company. Accountants are meticulous by instinct, and it goes against the grain to be slipshod; but it is not difficult, in shying away from the slipshod, to veer into the pedantic.

The question of materiality is really quite simple, and may be stated thus: No change in a balance sheet or income statement can be worth making that will not, in some way, influence a prospective reader of the statement. There is no merit in refining information down unless the refinement will affect someone who is making a decision on the basis of what he finds in the statements. As already explained, general purpose statements can be expected to give only a broad, overall view, and extensive detail can be a hindrance rather than a help. Anyone who wishes to prove this can do so very easily by taking a published balance sheet and making switches between items—such as deducting $100,000 from inventory and from retained earnings. It will be found that relatively large amounts can be deducted or added to different items without really changing in any material way the resulting picture, and in this way an appreciation can be gained of how wide the limits of materiality are. Here again it can be seen that the concept of materiality resolves itself into a question of utility. An alteration to a statement is material if it will prove useful to someone making a decision—and not otherwise.

The perils of muddleheadedness

The stubborn persistence of the idea that there can be some merit in financial statements apart from service to the business world has dragged us pretty close to the edge of the pit. Our peril may be appreciated from this quotation:

> . . . There is something to be said also for a certain naiveté and simplicity in accounting practice. If accounts are bound to be untruths anyhow, as I have argued, there is much to be said for the simple untruth as against a complicated untruth, for if the untruth is simple, it seems to me that we have a fair chance of knowing what kind of an untruth it is. A known untruth is much better than a lie, and provided that the accounting rituals are well known and understood, accounting may be untrue but it is not lies; it does not deceive because we know that it does not tell the truth, and we are able to make our own adjustment in each individual case, using the results of the accountant as evidence rather than as definitive information.[5]

There is here apparently a philosophic acceptance of the shortcomings of the accountant's product. The suggestion that the accountant's statements should be relegated from being definitive information to mere evidence, if it means anything at all, can only mean that the accountant's results should be ignored. Here is an economist who would not bother about having the accountant's concept reconciled with his—he would simply abandon it. Indeed, if the concepts are not reconciled, it is hard to imagine any other final outcome than the abandonment of the accountant's statements. To suggest that they do not provide the statement user with the basic information he needs but somehow have a sort of subsidiary validity or corroborative usefulness must surely be muddleheaded.

Relative and absolute values

It has been stressed that we must accept fully the implications of the utility hypothesis. The most important impli-

[5] K. E. Boulding, "Economics and Accounting: The Uncongenial Twins," in W. J. Baxter and Sidney Davidson (eds.), *Studies in Accounting Theory* (London: Sweet & Maxwell, Ltd., Law Publishers, 1962).

cation of all is that we must deal with relative rather than absolute values.

This may be illustrated by considering the thorny and unsolved problem of fixed asset valuation. Until now the generally accepted basis has been historic cost—tempered by various sorts of revaluation when no other course seemed possible.

As this is one of the most unsatisfactory areas in all accounting, there has been much discussion (unfortunately all of it inconclusive) of better methods. Replacement values have been suggested, and also bases providing for adjustments for changes in price levels. The reformers have put forward a variety of proposals, all attempting to provide a more current appraisal.

If we are to reach agreement on fixed asset valuation, it will be only through acceptance of the fact that any method must be arbitrary. It is no use arguing on grounds of logic or absolute truth. What we want to decide is simply this: Which of the possible methods provides the most useful presentation now available? The merit of the method agreed on will simply be that it provides a generally more informative picture than other methods. We must, of course, accept the possibility that someone may devise a still better method at some later date.

Serious criticisms can be advanced against all known methods of fixed asset valuation, and we will never get anywhere as long as we confine ourselves to tabulating the drawbacks to each method. We must concentrate on weighing the relative merits.

To illustrate further the applicability of the utility criterion, consider the line of argument that might be followed in choosing between, say, the historical cost and the replacement value approach to fixed asset valuation.

The comparison of the two methods might run along somewhat the following lines. Replacement cost is not necessarily a theoretically logical basis for fixed asset valuation. Moreover, when it comes to practical application, it will soon be found that an attempt to work out replacement values in actual cases can lead to extremely difficult problems. Fixed assets in modern business usually do not get replaced: they get superseded by more modern equipment or types of construction. It would be quite easy to list a number of serious disadvantages to replacement accounting.

Historical costs, on the other hand, while relatively simple to determine (being based on actual transactions), are also open to objection—including the quite fundamental objection that they have absolutely no current significance to anyone. A great deal of importance has been attached to the fact that historical costs represent an opinion about the value of an asset that was, at one stage, backed up by hard cash. However, many properties have changed hands at prices far too high, or far too low, and there is not necessarily a genuinely objective valuation in the price at which a property once changed hands. Moreover, the passage of time can remove any significance that the purchase price might once have had.

Even without getting into a more lengthy discussion of the relative merits and demerits of historical and replacement costs, it can be concluded that the replacement value method has a quite overwhelming advantage in that, with all its faults and shortcomings, it at least makes some effort to reach a current valuation—while historical cost does not. The choice in this case may therefore be said to boil down to a choice between a significant figure based on opinion and a quite meaningless figure based on actual cash transaction.

To highlight the factors involved in the choice between historical and replacement costs, consider the case of an investment analyst approaching the study of a new company through a review of its financial statements. Would he learn more about the company from statements based on historical costs or statements based on replacement values? There might quite possibly be a divergence of opinion on this point, but it should be possible to get some sort of consensus. It is on a consensus of this sort that generally accepted accounting principles should be based; that is to say, a consensus on which of these alternative methods of presentation would be most helpful to someone reading the statement.

The thesis of this chapter may be summarized by saying that accounting is strictly utilitarian, it does not deal with absolute values, and it cannot be justified as a system operating in a vacuum under its own rules.

4

Accounting as the Language of Business

ACCOUNTING has been described as "the language of business," which is a profoundly significant definition throwing light on the whole process. It establishes the fact that accounting is essentially a system of communication. For those concerned with accounting reform, this is of tremendous importance because, in trying to tidy up the loose thinking that has retarded the introduction of better types of statements, it reminds us that we are dealing with a means of communication and not with a complex philosophic system or with some profound mystery. We are simply trying to devise better ways of providing information.

As we have seen, running any business is mainly an exercise in decision making, and thus in good communication. The recognition of financial statements as a language emphasizes their practical, fluid, tentative character. It suggests that changes and improvement are likely to come from experiments and the inspiration of those trying to communicate actual messages, rather than from a solemn conclave of experts discussing methods of presentation in theory.

It becomes further evident that no statement, however ingenious or logically put together, has any merit whatever unless it communicates useful information—that is to say, unless it helps someone to make a decision. In this sense, it can be seen that the proposition "accounting is language" is simply another corollary deriving from the basic principle of usefulness laboriously expounded in the preceding chapter.

It is important to notice another close analogy between accounting and language. Information must be interpreted to be used, and the interpretation can always be either right or wrong. Thus, when providing information, one must accept the fact that it may be misunderstood and therefore misused. By clarity of presentation misinterpretation may be made unlikely, but it will always remain a possibility. The important point is that when one sets out to provide financial information, he must attempt to avoid misinterpretation but, at the same time, must accept some risk that misinterpretation will nevertheless occur. The only alternative is not to provide any information at all.

There is in fact little need to warn accountants about the possibility of misinterpretation. They tend to fall over backwards in guarding against it.

The essentials of good communication

Good communications have, then, two objectives: positively, to provide useful information, and negatively, to guard against being misleading.

When we come to judge the adequacy of the conventional statements we now produce, we can at least be proud of the excellent job the accounting profession has done on the negative side—in guarding against anyone's being misled. Accountants have certainly been careful to warn of this danger. They have constantly reiterated that the balance sheet is not a valuation document, and should not be relied on in valuing investments—principally because it is a mixture of historical and current costs. It has been emphasized that no one should compare one set of statements with another too confidently, as the two statements may be prepared on quite different, but equally acceptable, principles. Everyone has been warned that accounting statements are not intended for use in predicting the future. Nor is there any guarantee that even an audited statement may not be fraudulent—the auditor's responsibility being simply to give his opinion on the basis of an examination of the statements he considers adequate. It has been carefully explained that many basic factors are not taken into consideration in financial statements and that they thus provide only a partial sort of picture of the company's operations. It is no wonder that George O. May used to protest that accountants have worried so much about the possibility of being misleading that they have forgotten the obligation to provide information.

In short, the entire energies of the accounting profession have, it might almost seem, been devoted to persuading people not to pay any attention to financial statements in any of the circumstances in which they might, one would have thought, reasonably have recourse to them.

It is fair to ask why such a negative view has been taken: why accountants have not set about producing better statements instead of dwelling on the inadequacies of the statements they do succeed in producing. There has, of course, actually been great concern in accounting circles over the shortcomings of current statements; a real effort has been made to devise better methods; and some progress has resulted. However, in view of the enormously difficult problems that management is facing today and the runaway momentum of change—continually accentuating these difficulties and introducing new ones—few would argue with the proposition that current statements are inadequate and are becoming more and more seriously so every day. Improvements in statement production are running well behind new requirements. Thus the gap between the statements we need and those we can produce is constantly growing wider. We need urgently to accelerate the process of improvement.

Part of the trouble is that much earnest and well-intentioned crusading has been misdirected through failure to adhere to the two basic propositions dwelt on so far in this study:

1. Utility is the sole and fundamental consideration in financial reporting.
2. Accounting is in its nature closely akin to language and any attempt to reform it must take this into account.

Before proceeding any further on our own crusade, let us examine previous crusades to learn what we can from them. Three serious approaches to reform can be distinguished:

1. The view that technical jargon is at the base of all our trouble.
2. The view that all our difficulties would be solved if we insisted on full disclosure.
3. The view that we must start by refining and clarifying philosophically the basic theory and concepts on which our statements are based.

Crusades in each of these areas have had a certain measure of success, but none of them tackle the heart of the problem. We must examine each of these approaches in somewhat more detail to establish their limitations and to point to the need of a more effective solution.

The attack on jargon

We may first consider the proposition that the basic trouble with financial statements is that they are written in a jargon that no one but an expert can understand.

There is a certain plausibility to starting from this point. If accounting is in essence a language, better results would surely ensue if statement wording was simplified and made more generally understandable.

A great deal of time and effort has in fact been devoted to trying to rewrite statements in simplified English. We here meet that sterling character, the small investor—sometimes known as the "average layman" or "uninformed shareholder." The small investor is pictured as one almost inconceivably inexperienced in business. He is confused by terms like "inventories" or "liabilities" which he considers hopelessly technical. The assumption is that if we could get rid of this kind of jargon, the small investor would be in a position to take the financial statements of a company and value its shares intelligently.

This idea is so obviously fallacious that it might seem unnecessary to bother about it. Surely to encourage anyone for whom a term like "assets" must be translated into "what we own" that there is any possibility of his valuing his investment (or, indeed, of his doing himself any good whatever) by looking at a summarized statement of assets, liabilities, and income, is quite irresponsible.

Consider for a moment, for contrast, the position of a competent general manager of a corporation, with complete access to all information and with an excellent training in the business. Now even such an ideally placed person will have difficulty in reaching conclusions about the value of the shares of his company. What chance, then, has someone divorced from the affairs of the corporation and, by definition, completely untrained in business to reach any rational conclusion about the value of shares by looking at a dozen or so summarized figures?

The following drama was written in an attempt to settle, once and for all, the preposterous notion that if statements were prepared in language beamed directly at the untutored investor, all our troubles would be over.

SCENE: The living room of the home of Mrs. Winnie Zilch, a widow whose husband has died recently leaving her 1,000 shares of Mutilated Products, Inc., 100 shares of Dilapidated Paper Limited and a modest annuity. As the curtain rises, Mrs. Zilch is discovered with Mr. Fred Clunk, a retired salesman. Mr. Clunk's parents have just "passed on," so he finds himself orphaned at the age of 67, thus constituting with Mrs. Zilch a representative cross-section of that large group of average shareholders, the widows and orphans, who must have recourse to financial statements to keep track of the companies in which they invest. As a matter of fact, in this instance the two friends are in the act of reviewing several sets of annual statements, in contemplation of a possible switch in investments.

WINNIE: It's awfully good of you to come over and help me with my investment problems, Fred.

FRED: Not at all, but you know I'm no hot-shot accountant. Always was on the sales side. Never could abide all that figuring that used to go on in the accounting department. Now if you are going to buy some United Larceny like this friend of mine I was telling you about advises, you will have to sell one of the stocks you now have.

WINNIE: (Cautiously) Why? I don't get it.

FRED: So you'll have some money to buy the other stock with. Now the first question is, which of the stocks should you sell? I've looked it up in the paper and I find Mutilated is selling at $3 a share and Dilapidated at $100.

WINNIE: Well that sounds easy enough I must say, we'll sell that miserable $3 stock.

FRED: Yeah, honey, but that's not the way you do it. We've got to study these here financial statements and figure out which one is the best to sell. Now first of all, here's the statement of Dilapidated.

WINNIE: Good gracious, Fred, surely you don't expect me to read that old black and white thing. Ugh! Looks like a card of condolence or something. Can't we start on the attractive one with the glossy cover and vista-chrome illustrations?

FRED: O.K., that's the one for Mutilated. (He hands it to her). Incidentally, I hear it won an Oscar in a big competition. Now the way I understand it, you start by reading the auditors' report.

WINNIE: (After thumbing dutifully through the booklet) There isn't one.

FRED: Don't be silly, they'd never have given them that Oscar if they forgot the auditors' report. (He looks over her shoulder.) See, here it is on this page headed "A Word of Reassurance from your Friendly Chartered Accountant."

WINNIE: So that's it. Certainly looks just fine to me. The way they've printed every second line in a different kind of type sure is cute, and it takes your mind off the dullness of what they're saying. Now what next?

FRED: Well—ah—ah, let's see, you ought to check on the sales.

WINNIE: (Poring over a page with a fierce effort at concentration) There weren't any.

FRED: That's impossible, they must have had some. All these big companies sell something.

WINNIE: No, I've been over this balance sheet carefully, twice, and they don't mention sales.

FRED: Here let me have a look at it. Now, let's see — — — — — ah, yes here they are. They call them "Amounts due from customers for goods purchased by them." That is some of their technical jargon—just means "sales." Well, seems like that's all right, way up from last year.

WINNIE: What's next?

FRED: Well we should make sure the balance sheet balances. An auditor friend of mine once told me that if the books don't balance, anything, just anything, can happen. (Looks at total assets and then total liabilities) Right to the exact dollar—never could understand how those fellows did it. Just a minute now here's a note, let's see what it says. (Reads) Oh-oh, this doesn't sound too good to me, it says no depreciation was provided during the year.

WINNIE: Well, what's wrong with that? Surely, you wouldn't want a company that goes on depreciating. Land sakes, poor dear George once bought a stock at $80 and it depreciated right down to nothing. He used to say it was the worst investment he ever did make.

FRED: Yeah, but I don't think this is quite the same thing. I remember one year my boss said we hadn't made much profit but that there had been a lot of depreciation—he seemed to be quite pleased about it, like it was a good thing.

WINNIE: Probably just trying to be cheerful to keep your spirits up.

FRED: (Dubiously) Probably. Anyway it says here that the company was incorporated under the laws of Ontario, and I don't imagine those guys stand for any nonsense. Now let's analyze the statements of Dilapidated Paper.

WINNIE: What, that dingy old thing? I just couldn't bring myself to read that.

FRED: O.K. Then you're satisfied with the Mutilated, eh? We can go ahead and sell that.

WINNIE: Yes, only if everything's so good and so satisfactory about it, why do we sell it?

FRED: (Trying to be patient) Well you want to get some of this United Larceny, don't you? They got some big government contracts and a fellow was telling me that if he had some shares, he sure wouldn't sell them. In fact he'd buy more. And he happens to be a personal friend of the general manager. He says anyone who bought it would double his money by next summer.

WINNIE: Double your money? Let's see 1,000 shares at $3 each is $30,000 and double this is $60,000. Say that would be just fine, go ahead and get me some of that United What's-its-name.

CURTAIN [1]

Accountants must not, of course, be unsympathetic to the very real problems of the small investor, but our duty to him is to persuade him to get advice from a competent investment analyst or, alternatively, to place his funds in one of the investment trusts organized to look after people in his position. The duty of the accounting profession is to provide the experts who give counsel or who run investment trusts with the best and most accurate technical data that can be produced.

If the small investor wants to find anything out for himself by studying financial statements, he must be prepared to learn not only something about the art of financial reporting, but also about the operations of large business corporations. The figures in a set of financial statements are mainly useful as a point of enquiry for further investigations, rather than as a basis for facile generalizations, even by an expert. For example, an increase in sales may normally be considered a "good thing" but is there much value in this sort of casual judgment? Such sales increase may be the result of purchasing an unprofitable subsidiary, and thus may not be at all a "good thing." In valuing investments,

[1] Howard Ross, C.A., "Oscars—Consolation for the Losers," *The Canadian Chartered Accountant* (The Canadian Institute of Chartered Accountants), July, 1956.

there may be useful rules of thumb, but it is dangerous to assume that there is any easy road to investment valuation.

Incidentally, while jargon can be used to excess, and can be very irritating, it nevertheless has proper uses. It may provide a sort of shorthand in which experts can talk to each other more precisely and more conveniently than in common terms. For example, "amounts owing to us" may be a fair translation of "accounts receivable," but the term "accounts receivable" has for the accountant a certain precise technical significance that is lost in more generalized language. An account receivable is not only an amount owing, but one that arose in the course of business, that falls due on a specified basis, and that is stated at its estimated collectible value.

The fact that simple language does not necessarily convey clear ideas can be illustrated by reference to other disciplines. In this regard philosophy provides many excellent examples. A particularly admirable illustration, because it deals with a subject that accountants might feel they can aspire to understand, is found in Bertrand Russell's definition of number. Here we find him saying:

> Many philosophers, when attempting to define number, are really setting to work to define plurality, which is quite a different thing. Number is what is characteristic of numbers, as man is what is characteristic of men. A plurality is not an instance of number, but of some particular number. A trio of men, for example, is an instance of the number 3, and the number 3 is an instance of number; but the trio is not an instance of number.[2]

It is interesting to know that, although this is not a particularly easy passage to follow, the author goes on to say,

[2] Bertrand Russell, *Introduction to Mathematical Philosophy* (London: George Allen & Unwin, 1919), p. 11. (Also by The Macmillan Co., Publishers, New York.)

"This point may seem elementary and scarcely worth mentioning."

The interesting thing about this quotation is that it comes from an author with a high reputation for lucid writing, who has campaigned for years to rescue philosophy from those who would make it a jumble of incomprehensible jargon. There are no words in this quotation difficult to understand, but this does not mean the author's message is necessarily easy to grasp. This is the case with financial reporting. Knowing what the words mean is only a very small part of understanding the position the statements disclose. To someone wholly unversed in business, a set of financial statements cannot reveal the position of a complex modern corporation.

Thus, while there is everything to be said in favour of writing good clear English, and for getting rid of unnecessary jargon, the cause of good financial reporting is not very far advanced by a crusade aimed at having financial statements prepared in a public relations expert's notion of "good plain English"—itself a species of jargon.

More disclosure?

We may now turn to the efforts of those who have concentrated on the need for fuller disclosure. Here the implication is that if everything is fully disclosed, a clear picture of the company's operations will emerge. This again is arguable. Certainly, reasonable disclosure is necessary, and business men are often far too coy in the amount of information they consider they can safely give out.

The Securities and Exchange Commission, in the United States, has placed great emphasis on this aspect of financial reporting, and almost everyone would admit that a great deal of progress has been made in financial reporting by the Commission's insistence on greater disclosure. For example, the disclosure of the sales figure represents an important step forward. Any attempt to analyse a set of financial statements must be completely farcical without a sales figure. Nevertheless, the global figure of sales can be misleading. The total sales of large corporations are commonly a mixture of all sorts of different items, and any serious analysis must go far beyond the simple figure of total sales before any conclusions can be safely reached.

While the campaign for greater disclosure has been helpful, there are obvious limits to how much can be done by simply grinding out figures. In one of his detective stories, G. K. Chesterton makes the point that the easiest place to hide a leaf is in a forest, and that the easiest place to hide a dead leaf is in a pile of dead leaves. Disclosure has sometimes been stressed to the point where a massive amount of information is provided, from which it is extremely difficult to extract any really significant conclusions.

The stage is now set for a story from experience. Once upon a time there were ten competing manufacturers who were being investigated by a government department. Each was requested to provide certain information about its operations. Nine of the manufacturers gave the information grudgingly, being careful to provide precisely what was asked for (and therefore had to be provided) and nothing more. The tenth manufacturer, with a semblance of great zeal and cooperativeness, fairly snowed the department under with information. For example, where a simple breakdown of inventories among finished goods, work-in-process, and raw materials was requested, this company would provide full listings of individual inventory items, with details of cost adjustments and other technical calculations. Almost daily, new data would be sent in. If the man who conducted this investigation is still around, he would probably confirm that he obtained a clearer picture of the operations of the nine grudging manufacturers than of the wily tenth.

As we have said, what we need is a relatively few significant figures, properly calculated and clearly stated. A proliferation of irrelevant detail may serve only to obscure the picture. Moreover, a certain sense of proportion must be maintained. To refine the presentation in certain areas is useless if it must remain rough in more important areas. The added refinement of figures may be worse than useless: it may actually be distracting. Thus, if in a balance sheet the inventory is by far the largest and most significant figure, it is of little help to give the prepaid expenses in great detail. In the presentation of the cash position, a single net balance of all deposits and overdrafts is what is most often required. A detailed listing of deposits and overdrafts in various accounts is almost certain to be confusing rather than helpful.

It probably is generally true that analysts, working with a set of financial statements, spend more time grouping together items that have been patiently sorted out in the preparation of the statement than in breaking down figures into greater detail; because a general overall view is all that can be expected from a balance sheet and income statement. This whole question of overdisclosure ties in with the "materiality corollary" discussed in the preceding chapter. Additional detail that does not affect the general picture (which is all that the statements provide) is undesirable.

Perhaps the matter can be reduced to a general rule: that providing information is helpful only if someone uses the information. There is no merit in providing information for its own sake. In fact, information that is not going to be used is worse than useless: it tends to clutter up and divert.

In short, further disclosure simply cannot be the full answer to improvement in financial reporting. That it has already been overstressed is highly probable. It certainly does not need further emphasis.

Philosophic musings

Another and perhaps more serious crusade has been the attempt to refine accounting definitions and terms. In this sort of philosophic approach, we find ourselves being introduced (as explained in a previous chapter) to "postulates" and "principles" and "conventions" and "procedures." On the face of it, it seems plausible to object to looseness in terminology and lack of agreement on basic matters. It worries many accountants that they are expected to report that statements are "in accordance with generally accepted accounting principles" when it is cheerfully admitted that no one can draw up an authoritative list of the principles supposed to be generally accepted.

A philosopher would presumably approach the problem by attempting to discover and state the fundamental principles. This appears to be the accepted technique in philosophic investigation and we may assume it is appropriate in that field; but has this sort of approach any validity in accounting? Nothing can be more wrong-headed than adopting techniques appropriate in other fields without first being sure they are also appropriate in the new field to which they are applied. In the philosopher's unending search for truth, it might be expected that when one philosopher has made a profoundly searching investigation and emerges with a statement of basic truths, the next philosopher would build on this foundation. This is not how it seems to work however. Instead, each succeeding philosopher devotes himself to criticism of what has already been done, hoping he can destroy the foundations already set up and dig down deeper into the riddle of truth. This sort of thing can easily be observed in any standard philosophic text; each new thinker probes more deeply than his predecessor and progress is, as it were, backwards.

This kind of searching analysis of basic beliefs may sound like a useful approach to any subject. Actually, in accounting, it is almost inconceivable that it will produce results fast enough. It may even be doubted whether this intellectual kind of refinement has anything to do with such a rough-and-ready, tentative undertaking as the preparation of financial statements.

An illustration of the philosophic approach may be found in an excellent study produced recently by the then Research Director of the American Institute of Certified Public Accountants under the title of *The Basic Postulates of Accounting*. This study sets down propositions that sound basic enough, such as these:

Quantification. Quantitative data are helpful in making *rational economic decisions,* i.e., in making choices among alternatives so that actions are correctly related to consequences.

Entities. Economic activity is carried on through specific units or entities.

Time Period. Economic activity is carried on during specifiable periods of time.

Unit of Measure. Money is the common denominator in terms of which the exchangeability of goods and services, including labor, natural resources, and capital, are measured.[3]

[3] Maurice Moonitz, Ph.D., C.P.A., *Accounting Research Study No. 1* (New York: American Institute of Certified Public Accountants, 1961), pp. 21–22.

Profound as these postulates are, it is interesting to find that one criticism of this study is that it does not probe back far enough into the basic objectives of accounting. For example, in a commentary printed as part of this Research Study, we find Leonard Spacek, C.P.A., saying:

> In my opinion, this monograph does not adequately describe the real purpose and objectives of accounting, and the concepts set forth as being postulates cannot provide a basic foundation from which to build a sound framework of accounting theory.[4]

Moreover, the study can also be criticized from the point of view that some of the basic postulates, however axiomatic they may sound, are difficult and perhaps even impossible to apply in actual practice.

Basic communication

Three approaches to financial statement reform have now been reviewed—simplified language, greater disclosure, and refinement of concepts. While each of these approaches may contribute something of value, it would seem evident that, even in combination, they are quite inadequate in coping with the really difficult problem of improving financial reporting.

The right approach to producing better statements is to emphasize the simple proposition with which this chapter started out—namely, that accounting is essentially a language or a means of communication. The analogy with language can be carried quite far. For example, we seem to have achieved reasonable agreement on what is good and bad grammar—but when we set out to list the rules of grammar we immediately provoke argument. In fact, the only

[4] *Ibid.*, p. 58.

people who have any real confidence in their grasp of the rules of grammar are the semi-literate. The more scholarly and experienced are less dogmatic about hard-and-fast grammatic rules, illustrating Dr. George Shortt's theory that "education is a process whereby one progresses from cocksure ignorance to thoughtful uncertainty."

Yet with all the basic uncertainties and arguments about grammar, we nevertheless contrive to communicate with each other reasonably effectively. This should encourage us to hope that we may be able to develop better financial statements while still admitting to a certain haziness in regard to our basic concepts.

The language analogy may perhaps be pressed one step further. In grammar there are many authorities who doubt the usefulness of a codification of rules. In his preface to his authoritative "The King's English," H. W. Fowler points out—

> It is notorious that English writers seldom look into a grammar or composition book; the reading of grammars is repellent because, being bound to be exhaustive on a greater or less scale, they must give much space to the obvious or the unnecessary.[5]

Fowler proceeds on a different, and very successful, tack by including in his book only the confusing questions which cause the trouble. This is in fact a technique that accounting bodies have been inclined to follow. They have not been very happy in their tentative efforts at a general statement of what accounting principles are—but they have succeeded in producing many satisfactory pronouncements on specific points that have given rise to practical difficulties. In the neighbouring field of auditing, for example, there has not

[5] H. W. Fowler, *The King's English* (London: Oxford University Press, 1906), p. 3.

been a satisfactory general pronouncement on audit procedures, but there have been good bulletins on specific points—such as the necessity of circularization in the audit of receivables and of physical inspection in the audit of inventories. Perhaps this indicates the most suitable approach to clarification in the field of financial reporting.

To get back to the comparison of accounting and language, let us consider how we might go about a crusade to improve the writing of English. No doubt leading authors and literary critics would be appealed to for help—but we would surely not suppose that the standard of writing could be improved by getting together a cross-section of authors and critics and asking them to draw up an agreed code of rules on good writing. Efforts to make progress in this way in accounting have, not too surprisingly, produced meagre results.

It is interesting to speculate on the persistence of the theoretical accountant's obsession with the problem of codification. In what other disciplines is it attempted? The law is codified in some countries, but other countries seem to get on just as well on common law principles without benefit of a code. Moreover the legal codes that do exist deal with a relatively slow changing subject. The revision of a legal code is a huge, ponderous undertaking. It is hard to conceive of the successful application of the codification idea to anything as rapidly changing as commercial practice—and that is what a code of accounting principles would require.

The measure of our failure to remember that accounting is essentially a means of communication is that, as already suggested, successful business executives quite commonly accept the notion that the financial statements of a company can only really be understood by professional accountants.

The executive has no reason to study, and no need to understand, the technical procedures that go into statement preparation. This is the proper domain of the trained accountant. But the end product—the statement—is prepared for the executive. If he does not understand it, there is little comfort in knowing that the accountants do, and that it has been prepared in accordance with a systematic set of rules which the executive would subscribe to if he understood them.

5

Confusion and Complication

IT IS THE essential theme of this book that financial reporting is a relatively simple and straightforward art. We should never allow it to become complicated or abstruse. In previous chapters we have attempted to concentrate on a basic train of thought: that as financial statements are prepared solely to provide information, they are satisfactory only when they provide as much useful information as possible and provide it as clearly and unambiguously as possible.

The great problem is not that these simple truths are challenged. They are, in fact, accepted. The trouble is that other considerations are allowed to confuse the issue.

Some of this confusion is predictable and understandable —arising naturally from the difficult nature of the task of developing good methods of communication—and some of it is curious and unexpected. In some instances it may be explained as the result of the sort of occupational distortion that develops inevitably in any profession. Certain qualities are required in the professional man—as, for example, caution and accuracy are in the accountant—and he develops such qualities. The distortion arises when these virtues are so drilled in that they get overemphasized and, being carried too far, become vices.

Satisfactory financial statements will never be produced until we purge ourselves of some persistent errors. It is now time to consider what these are.

How objective can you get?

One example of the occupational distortions of the accounting profession is the overemphasis on what is described as "objectivity." How essential objectivity really is in accounting depends on what is meant by the term. In its broadest and best sense, objectivity is an attitude of mind —the basic attitude of unprejudiced fairness required in any good judicial system.

In this sense, it is a quality that could hardly be overdone in accounting. It would be absurd to suggest that statements could be prepared too honestly or with too little personal bias. However, the trouble is that, in the pursuit of this admirable goal, we have extended the concept of objectivity to cover procedures that are "objective" in quite a different sense.

At best, financial statements must always be a combination of opinion and recorded fact. As opinions are clearly subjective, wherever they occur the possibility is open for the prejudices of the statement producer to enter. It is no wonder that accountants, with the heavy responsibility of preparing statements that are not misleading, tend to shy away from the introduction of opinion wherever it is possible to substitute for it something of a factual nature—something that does not depend on personal judgment.

Searching for solid data not dependent on anyone's unsupported opinion, accountants fastened on cash transactions, and concentrated much of their attention on devising ways of recording and analysing such transactions accurately. However, the simple statement of receipts and disbursements soon gave way to an income statement based on accruals, for while such accruals require estimation (and thus introduce a subjective element), they result in a more meaningful presentation. As a reasonably complete view of a business could not be produced entirely from cash receipts and expenditures, it was necessary to fill in gaps by estimates and opinions, but the tendency was to keep these to a minimum. Wherever there was a choice between a figure based on a cash transaction and one that was not, the former was preferred.

In pursuit of objectivity, accountants thus came to venerate cash transactions. They felt that the purchase of an asset represented an opinion backed by hard cash. This made the amount paid for an asset seem a more reliable indication of value than a simple appraisal unsupported by the laying out of cash. But while a cash transaction may be good evidence of value, it may also be misleading. To argue otherwise would be to suggest that no one has ever paid too much for anything and that no one has ever got a bargain.

While this type of objectivity has some merit, it is not so fundamental a consideration as are others with which it may sometimes conflict. Relevance, for example, is a much more basic virtue. A relevant valuation may sometimes be wrong, but an irrelevant one cannot possibly be of any use, no matter how objectively it is reached.

In the convenient illustration of historical and replacement costs, we are presented with a choice between an objective basis for valuing fixed assets and a subjective basis. Historical costs are supported by actual cash transactions. But if some of these transactions have taken place so many years ago that they are no longer significant, it is possible, and even likely, that a more useful picture can be presented by an opinion as to the current value of the assets—even though not supported by a cash transaction. Furthermore, it might be pointed out that in conventional fixed asset valuation, while the gross valuation of a fixed asset is solidly grounded on an actual cash transaction, this gross valuation is not what matters. The important consideration is the net or depreciated value. This net valuation must be reached by estimating the proper number of years over which the cost of the asset should be written off. Under the accountant's rule of matching expenses against revenues, this means estimating the prospective useful life of the asset; and strictly speaking it should require a calculation of the extent to which each year of this useful life has benefited through use of the asset. This becomes a most complicated calculation —not to say an impossible one. Not only are there the difficult (and necessarily theoretical) calculations of wear and tear, but there has to be considered the even more completely unpredictable factor of obsolescence. Consequently in practice, there is inevitably recourse to very rough-and-ready assumptions regarding useful life. It has been very common in Canada, for example, to use a depreciation rate of 10 per cent (straight line) for all sorts of machinery and equipment. No one could pretend this is anything but exceedingly arbitrary. Thus, while in conventional fixed asset accounting we start out with a value based on a cash transaction, in the end the significant figure of net depreciated value contains a very important element of estimation.

Still another element of dubiety in cash transactions is the question of the genuineness of the transaction. For a cash transaction to have any validity at all, it must be a transaction involving a bona fide change of ownership. Here enter further difficulties. A corporation is a legal person and theoretically its assets belong to it, and not to the shareholders.

Thus a sale of property between any two corporations is, in the eyes of the law, a valid sale regardless of the ownership of the two corporations. However, in common sense, if the two corporations are owned by the same people, a sale between them can take on a certain artificiality. The way is left open for easy manipulation. As the lawyers say, purchaser and seller are not dealing at arm's length.

The subject of arm's length transactions comes up frequently in income tax determination, and anyone familiar with its ramifications in that field can appreciate what almost insoluble problems can sometimes be involved in establishing whether a deal is at arm's length or not. It is always difficult for the tax authorities to distinguish between fraudulent non-arm's-length transactions and innocent dealings. The important conclusion, for purposes of the present discussion, is that reliance on cash transactions, as a basis for asset valuation, introduces all the difficulties that surround the arm's length concept.

To illustrate finally the ultimate absurdity of adhering to cash transactions in the pursuit of objectivity, let us consider the actual case history of a pair of identical semi-detached residences. One of the residences was last sold in 1943 for $6,000 and the other in 1963 for $36,000. This may seem an amazing variation, but it represented the depressed real estate market in the area during World War II and the present boom conditions. In any event, it is the principle that is important and everyone can recognize the common situation in which identical assets sell at different prices at different times.

Consider now the conventional treatment of these residences in their owners' balance sheets in 1963. The owner of the second house would carry it at $36,000. On the other hand, if the owner of the first house uses the popular straight-line rate of depreciation for buildings of 2½ per cent, his residence would appear in his balance sheet at $3,000. If the sale at $36,000 was a legitimate one, can it possibly be justifiable to carry the first house at $3,000? Does this value mean anything to someone who is trying to use a balance sheet to find out something about the owner's financial position? If the houses are identical, is not the $36,000 valuation just as much an appraisal backed by cash as the $3,000 figure? To drive home the full preposterousness of our conventional treatment, it might be pointed out that if both these residences had been purchased by the same owner, it would be considered quite proper for him to carry the two identical assets—one at a valuation of $3,000 and the other at $36,000 in his balance sheet. Moreover, if he sold the first house subsequently for $30,000 it would be considered that he should record a $27,000 capital gain, whereas if he sold the second house at that price he would register a $6,000 capital loss. This is all systematic, consistent, and tidy, but who would claim it makes sense?

Even the most inflexible of accountants would perhaps not carry conventional procedures to their logical conclusion when dealing with a case as extreme as this. In practice some way can usually be found to soften such absurdities as permitting the owner of two identical fixed assets to carry one of them at twelve times the value of the other. But this is not the point. It is all very well to devise some means of adjustment (through appraisal, write-down, averaging-up, or something of the sort) when one comes face to face with a transparently grotesque situation. The significant conclusion is that even if one owner does not have two identical assets purchased at such different prices—even indeed if two identical assets do not exist—it would still be ridiculous for anyone to carry the first house in his balance sheet in 1963 at $3,000. If there were no current sale of an identical house to go by, surely some more intelligent value than $3,000 could be established. What does it matter if one appraiser valued the house at $30,000 and another at $40,000 (a spread that might be considered improbably wide in practice)? Either of these figures is nearer the mark than $3,000.

In the foregoing case the problem is indeed simplified by the current sale of an identical property. Often, perhaps normally, things will not work out that conveniently. However, if there is not an identical house, there are usually reasonably similar houses. If there is not a recent scale, there is at least a reasonably demonstrable market. Whatever the problems are, it must be rarely that a twenty-year-old transaction provides the best basis available for valuation.

The most important general criticism of financial statements, as we now produce them, is not that they are inaccurate, nor that there is anything illogical about the generally accepted accounting principles on which they are based; the most general criticism is simply that the financial statements are not sufficiently informative.

We have gone too far in our devotion to objectivity. If better statements are to be produced, they can be produced only by improving the quality of judgment that goes into their preparation—not by resisting so fanatically the extension of the judgmental element. The essential task of the accounting profession is to encourage the use of the most impartial and best-informed opinions that can be brought to bear.

To sum up, the trouble with overrating objectivity is that it tends to make us satisfied with a valuation that can be documented and thus defended, rather than encouraging us to develop more realistic and useful valuation procedures.

Sins in the name of conservatism

Accountants have a deeply imbedded predilection for what they call "conservatism." This springs naturally from the heavy responsibilities that anyone assumes who has to issue the financial statements of a large public corporation. Moreover, credit was perhaps originally the most important purpose for which statements were produced. In fact for many years, the balance sheet was the only annual statement that got much attention. In these circumstances it was natural that the principal concern of accountants was to avoid overstating assets or understating liabilities.

Understandable as this attitude was when financial statements were used principally for credit purposes, the bias towards conservatism becomes completely invalid once attention is focused on income determination—as it has been now for quite some time. For example, a typical act of "conservatism" is to charge as much as possible to expense rather than to capital. This does produce a "conservative" balance sheet. Also, it produces a conservative income statement in the year in which the expenses are written off; but in subsequent years it increases the amount of profit shown in the income statement, which is the reverse of "conservatism" as the term is used by accountants. Another illustration is provided by inventory values. An understatement of the value of the inventory does produce a conservative balance sheet (and also a conservative income statement in the current year), but any reduction in inventory value has the effect of increasing the profits shown in the following year's statements.

Quite apart from such considerations, every time shares of a large corporation change hands, there must be both a seller and a purchaser. It is all very well to protect the purchaser by being sure that the financial statements he examines do not overstate profitability; but a precisely similar obligation exists to the vendor of the shares, in that he must not be persuaded to value the shares he is selling too low by financial statements that understate profits. It is this that leads to the severest and most legitimate criticism when companies are taken over at less than their real value, simply because their financial statements have underrated profitability.

Yet another criticism of the accountant's tendency to conservatism is that, whatever merit it might have once had, any value in conservatism is to a large extent now lost because, once the conservative propensities of accountants became generally recognized, the results they reported were interpreted accordingly. It is today automatically assumed by everyone that financial statements understate profits—a most unsatisfactory situation. The reader is left to guess at the degree of conservatism, and may end up by adding back what he supposes to have been too conservatively written off. When we arrive at this stage, a set of financial statements has lost most of its value.

A homely illustration of the bad effect of our bias towards understatement of values is provided by the example of someone who always sets his alarm clock fifteen minutes fast. This may be effective in getting him up early for a few mornings but, as anyone who has tried it will find out, the advance is soon subconsciously discounted. To provide a full parallel to the effect of conservatism in accounting, a better illustration would be an alarm clock set each day by someone who is instructed to set it ahead of time by varying amounts undisclosed to the sleeper. The sleeper would then be pretty much in the position of someone reading a financial statement today. He can safely assume the clock is fast but has no way of figuring out by how much.

In short, whatever merit the practice of conservatism might once have had, in today's business world it has none. The accountant's real responsibility is not to be sure everything is understated; it is to present a fair and unbiased picture. He should be protected when he has used his best skill and care in arriving at the judgments necessary to produce a proper statement, and it should be unnecessary for him to distort the position conservatively to protect himself against the possibility that some of the valuations will prove, through hindsight, to have been too optimistic.

Conservatism is not like objectivity, a virtue that has been sometimes carried too far. In fact it is the reverse of objectivity. It suggests that the accountant should use his judgment in deliberately understating values.

The accountant has somewhat similar problems to a Judge attempting to assess the amount of damages in a court case. The Judge must determine damages at an amount that will be fair to plaintiff and to defendant. He cannot "play it safe" by setting damages that are certainly not too high, so as to be sure he is not being unfair to the defendant, and vice versa. The accountant has much the same obligation to be fair to both buyer and seller.

The most difficult application of conservatism to get rid of will be the sacred dogma that anticipated losses should be recognized but that profit must never be taken up until actually "realized." This principle is enshrined, for example, in the notion that inventories should be valued at the lower of cost or market, but even this apparently safe and cautious rule has had its day.

Tackling a proposition as firmly entrenched as lower-of-cost-or-market is a serious business. It will get us nowhere to obtain consent to the general proposition that statements must not be understatements, if this is assented to with any mental reservation. It is not good enough for an accountant to concede that an overstatement should be considered as serious a distortion as an understatement, if he in fact goes on worrying about the uncertainties of life and, when he comes up against a hard practical decision, slips back into the position that it would be prudent to provide for prospective losses, but imprudent to assume that profits, of a similar degree of likelihood, were in fact going to be realized. We have had plenty of lip service of this sort where people say the right things but do the wrong.

In order that no speakers of weasel words will have any shred of cover to hide behind, we must spend a moment examining this aspect of accounting in some detail.

To start with, let us consider the simple and clear-cut example of readily marketable securities held as an investment of surplus funds. In the ordinary course of many businesses large sums may be invested for considerable periods of time. For example, the characteristic pattern of a newspaper company results from the need to make a very large investment in a new press every thirty years or so. The company therefore goes through long periods when funds are slowly accumulated to meet this recurring major obligation. In this and other ways, ordinary non-investment businesses often hold marketable securities and consequently make very appreciable profits or losses. How should these be accounted for to provide the clearest information?

Take the case of a company that invests $10,000 in shares of A Company in 1959 and let us suppose the market value of such shares rises so that at December 31 for a period of years the market value of the shares is as follows:

1959—$11,000
1960— 14,000
1961— 16,000

1962—$21,000
1963— 23,000
1964— 24,000

and let us suppose also that the shares are sold in 1965 for $25,000. Conventional accounting would require the investment to be carried at $10,000 through this period. The market value would be shown parenthetically, the effect being that no profit would be taken up in any year until 1965, and a profit of $15,000 would be reported as earned in that year. Can anyone pretend this is reasonable? For example, at the end of 1962, why should it not be recognized that the Company owns an asset worth $21,000 and that it has earned $5,000 on the investment during the year? It could be argued that this gain is uncertain and would be lost if the shares dropped in price before being sold. But another company could buy the same shares in 1962 for $21,000 and be entitled to carry them at that figure, in spite of the fact that it is exposed to precisely the same risk.

This case illustrates the great truth investors have to learn so painfully: once you have made an investment, what you have paid ceases to matter. You are concerned only with what is going to happen to the price of your shares next.

Marketable securities provide a nice clean uncomplicated example of the total unsuitability of cost as a basis of asset valuation. When we move on to a consideration of inventories of merchandise, we encounter a whole raft of new factors. There are questions of deterioration, of obsolescence, of quantity discounts, of handling charges, and location—each one of which makes the valuation less clean-cut and more tentative. Still further difficulties arise in manufacturing when goods must be dealt with at various stages of production. However, none of these complicating factors in any way mitigate the underlying absurdity of the cost basis.

It is well recognized that when the market price of inventoried goods drops, it is appropriate to record the resulting loss. There can be no sane conclusion other than a recognition that if the opposite happens and prices rise, a profit should be recorded. This is no more imprudent or risky than continuing to carry the goods at cost if prices remain unchanged. In the latter case, too, there is a risk of loss if prices subsequently drop.

Of course no one would suggest that the goods in inventory should be written up to the company's selling price and all the profit be thus attributed to the period in which the goods were purchased. The appropriate market for valuing the inventory is the company's purchase price, and a profit should be taken up only when this price has risen. Here again, marketable securities afford the simplest situation as there is only one market (disregarding brokerage), while for merchandise there can be various markets, such as manufacturer's, wholesale and retail. The important thing to hold on to through all these complexities is that there can be no rational determination of income on any basis other than current valuation—however complicated, however rough.

If we are to succeed in the difficult task of adding together apples and oranges, by reducing all types of asset to money equivalent, the key objective must be to state each asset at the least amount of money for which a sensible proprietor would be prepared to exchange it.

The Frankenstein of double-entry bookkeeping

The system of double-entry bookkeeping is at the very foundation of modern accounting, going back at least to the Franciscan monk Paciolo and his famous treatise on bookkeeping published in Italy in 1494.

First let it be said that double-entry bookkeeping is a simply marvellous invention. There is something fascinating about the symmetry of debits and credits, which establishes so clearly the fact that any business transaction has two sides which can be recorded and balanced. Double-entry bookkeeping provides a wonderful automatic control in the compilation of figures. It is a magnificent statistical tool. However, we must remember that it is a statistical tool, and we must not try to pretend that it is anything more than that.

The double-entry system does not add anything to the data processed through it. It has nevertheless obsessed accountants; and this to the extent that when an item is mentioned to an accountant, his first instinctive question to himself is apt to be "What is the other side of the entry?" In short, while double-entry bookkeeping is an extremely useful device, it has gained an exaggerated and false position of dominance in accounting thought. A valuable "means" has become an "end" in itself.

The concentration on the bookkeeping aspects of accounting has resulted in a tendency for the study of financial statements to be approached from the point of view of accounting procedures. This tendency is all the more natural (and dangerous) because, as we have seen previously, the characteristic job of an accountant is to prepare a statement rather than to use it. Thus accountants have been absorbed in the mechanics of statement preparation and have not paid enough attention to the needs of a person who wants to use the statements.

The users normally lack the technical knowledge of statement production necessary to enable them to criticize effectively. They simply get a statement inadequate for their purposes. If they complain at all, they are apt to be told that technical considerations preclude a more informative presentation, and they have no way of finding out whether this is true or not. They are in the accountants' hands.

Undoubtedly one of the facts that has prevented more progress in statement preparation is the unfortunate break that occurs between the preparation and use of statements. Most accountants lose interest in a statement once it has been prepared; while the users of the statement are usually in no position to insist on statements that would answer their requirements better because they do not know what improvements are technically feasible.

It is unlikely that we will get better statements if we start with a study of procedures. These are already drilled into apprentice accountants so fiercely that we have developed a group of technicians absorbed in the intricacies of statement preparation. With this approach, the tendency is to set up accounting procedures and to see what sort of statement they produce. It is not surprising to find that some accountants appear to consider the main problem in statement preparation to be the systematic disposal, on a consistent basis from year to year, of the balances thrown up by the double-entry bookkeeping system.

We would have made more progress if we had started by considering the requirements of those who use financial statements, and when these had been clearly and firmly established, we had then turned our attention to devising the sort of statistical procedures that would produce such results. Obviously the double-entry principle will always be basically important and useful, but it should be servant and not master.

It must be emphasized again that the function of the accountant is not to give managers, investors, and creditors the figures the accountants consider they should want. The function of the accountant is, rather, to understand the problem of these groups and to work out ways of giving them what they actually do want. It follows, as a corollary, that it is also the accountant's function to make sure that those who need financial statements are aware of the different types of statement that can be produced to help them.

The obsession of accountants with double-entry techniques is their contribution to the traditional misunderstanding between accountants and economists. Undoubtedly economists too contribute to these misunderstandings—generally through making impractical demands for information.

The devotion of accountants to double entry is neatly illustrated by their attitude to depreciation. Depreciation accounting is simply a systematic amortization of capital costs. Ordinary current costs the accountant disposes of simply by writing them off against revenue. It is manifestly wrong to write off against one year's revenue major costs that will "benefit" a number of years. These are the so-called capital costs and the accountant disposes of them by assuming a useful life for the assets and writing them off over such assumed period.

Capital costs are thus neatly and systematically disposed of and, in the process, the accountant gets around to persuading himself that his basic function is to match costs against revenues. He thus sidetracks problems of valuation by announcing that the purpose of accounting is not valuation at all, but rather the matching of costs and revenues. That this is simply an evasion of his manifest responsibility will be argued in a later chapter.

The doubtful legacy of the joint venture concept

Not all the errors that take root in our thinking are such large fundamental concepts. Sometimes relatively minor considerations have deflected the progress of accounting with long-term effect. As an illustration of this sort of thing, we might consider joint ventures. The emergence of joint ventures was one of the factors that first aroused interest in financial statements. When a number of people went into a venture together, it became absolutely essential to determine how much profit had been made, so that this could be properly shared amongst the participants.

Historically joint ventures became popular before anyone had thought of the limited liability company, with its wonderful adaptability and possibilities for growth. The joint stock companies in fact developed out of experience with joint ventures when the scale of enterprise had grown so large that simple joint ventures were inadequate.

However a joint venture is quite different from a modern corporation. It is for a limited, usually a quite short, period of time. Normally there are relatively few contributors, and they engage in simple operations—such as the purchase of goods to be resold, with a subsequent sharing out of profits. The first serious profit and loss accounts were developed to serve such ventures.

When the more complicated joint stock company was developed, financial statements for joint ventures were adapted to such new organizations. One of the essential differences between a limited liability company and a joint venture is that the former is organized for an indefinitely long-term existence. Indefinite existence is thus one of the basic assumptions in preparing statements for companies—the so-called going concern concept. Another fundamental difference is that companies are set up with the specific intention of making their shares readily transferable.

The facts of continued existence and transferability introduce a fundamentally new problem: the production of periodic statements. To produce such statements it becomes necessary to attribute income and expenses to specific periods. This in turn leads to the necessity of distinguishing between capital expenditures that benefit several periods and expenses that benefit only one period. This basic distinction does not enter into accounting for joint ventures of limited duration, but by inventing such devices as the amortization of the cost of "fixed" assets, joint venture accounting was developed into accounting for corporations. While joint ventures have long ceased to be of any great importance, the early influence of joint venture accounting has persisted amazingly, perhaps because it provides such a convenient introduction to corporate accounting in teaching. Each succeeding generation of accountants thus continues to think of corporate accounting as an extension of joint venture accounting. This has a strong influence on, for example, the profession's addiction to historical cost in fixed asset valuation.

Historical costs are clearly right in joint ventures, the profit or loss on the venture being the difference between what the owners paid in and what they received back; but when we come to consider the operations of large, modern, publicly owned corporations, we find these have almost no resemblance to joint ventures. Their statements should take into account the key fact that shares of the corporation are continually changing hands on the market. The ownership of corporations is thus constantly changing and the historical cost of the fixed assets is likely to have little or no significance to the current owners. What they are interested in is the value of a corporation at the time they purchase their shares and the value when they sell. In other words, the current values. The terminal realizable value of the assets is equally irrelevant because shareholders get in and out without the corporation being wound up.

In certain circumstances, this aspect of corporate accounting becomes so obvious that accountants recognize it. For example, when a company acquires controlling interest in the stock of another company, accountants recognize the phenomenon of acquisition surplus. The surplus position is "frozen" at the date that control of the company is acquired. Only profits earned after acquisition are considered as earnings of the parent company.

Precisely the same principle should apply in logic to minority shareholdings as to control. While it would clearly be impractical to have a separate set of financial statements for each minority shareholder, it should nevertheless be realized that constantly shifting ownership introduces a significant new problem in accounting. When an investor buys shares of a corporation through the stock market, he pays a price that takes into account, amongst other things, the current value of its assets. For such an owner, the original cost of these assets is of no significance or interest. He was not a shareholder when they were bought. To him the only significant value is the value on the date he makes his investment in the corporation, not the value on the date the corporation acquired the assets.

The glittering but vulnerable mantle of infallibility

Honesty is so obviously a basic requirement in the preparation of financial statements and is so much stressed that its importance might at times seem almost exaggerated. Integrity certainly comes first in the qualities required of an accountant. A certain degree of intelligence is also desirable, but without integrity the production of a reliable statement cannot even be embarked on.

There is thus nothing wrong with insistence on integrity, but it can be undesirable to carry this insistence so far that the accountant gets to thinking he is supposed to be infallible. The danger is that if too much insistence is placed on an accountant's obligation to be honest, he may get to assuming that everything he says must be unchallengeably true, which is really quite another matter. This can result in a hesitance to say anything at all—and surely that cannot be the accountant's role. He is supposed to be a communicator of useful information.

The great danger here is that an accountant may tend to confine himself to using figures that are absolutely incontrovertible, however inadequate such figures may be, rather than venture more boldly into the opinion area, where he may be wrong but is nevertheless very likely to be right. Take the auditor's attitude to inventories over the years. It must first be admitted that the valuation and checking of inventories is one of the most difficult tasks an auditor has. Until relatively recently, the difficulties inherent in inventory valuation led the auditor to attempt to wash his hands of any responsibility for the inventory. The idea was promoted that the inventory was peculiarly management's responsibility. In one or two court cases, it was held that the auditor was not an appraiser or valuer, and auditors hid behind such decisions—in spite of the fact that the inventory is frequently one of the most important items in a set of financial statements. To report that a statement presents a fair view, while disclaiming any responsibility for the inventory figure, is quite unsatisfactory.

It would certainly have been preferable if auditors had earlier recognized the obvious necessity to interest themselves in the correctness of the inventory valuation, realizing that all anyone has a right to expect from them is the use of honesty, skill, and due care.

A reputation for infallibility, if taken seriously by the auditor himself, can prevent him from doing a useful job. The notion that people expect him to be infallible also encourages the auditor to shy away from responsibilities, under the impression that these responsibilities are more onerous than they actually are. Once the idea is seized on that the auditor is not expected to be some sort of paragon, but simply an ordinary skilled professional man, doing the best he can, the work of substantiating a statement with a professional opinion becomes much easier to tackle.

The wonderfully precise balancing of the two sides of a balance sheet must appear to many to be one of the chief mysteries and glories of the art of accounting. But this absolute balance of assets and liabilities frequently gives a misleading impression of accuracy. How can anyone but an accountant be expected to know that asset valuations are rough approximations when there is such a tidy and impressive balancing of total assets and liabilities?

Legal concepts

Most accounting text books emphasize statutory requirements and the precepts established by court cases, in the preparation of financial statements. Some attention, of course, must be paid to such legal provisions. In the early days of limited liability, when the business world was wrestling with this exciting new invention, legal aspects of financial statements must have loomed large. Sir William Gilbert, himself a lawyer, was setting Sullivan the problem of putting limited liability to music:

> You start by a declaration of the extent
> To which you intend to pay your debts.
> This is known as your stated capital.[1]

[1] From the opera *Utopia Limited* by Gilbert and Sullivan, which opened in London in 1893.

However, legal requirements, whether embodied in statutes or court decisions, can only follow and attempt to consolidate business practices. For example, the requirements in regard to financial presentation in statutes can hardly go beyond generally accepted accounting principles. In fact it is customary, and perhaps wise, for the legal requirements to follow at some distance behind the generally accepted principles developed by business men and accountants in the course of their work, while in financial presentation we must always be developing and breaking new ground. There is no way a good statute could be drafted other than by following good established practice. One of the key considerations in statute requirements is to provide adequate disclosure; but as to what constitutes adequate disclosure, there can be no guide other than what someone has found in practice to be helpful or essential.

The law courts have precisely the same problem. When a judge is attempting to decide a question relating to financial statements, he must spend most of his time trying to find out what good business practice is. How else could he logically decide the case? As Mr. Justice Locke said in a famous tax case:

> Neither of the statutes defines the manner in which manufacturing costs of this nature are calculated and, in the absence of such determination, they are to be determined, in my opinion, upon the ordinary principles of commercial trading.[2]

As statutory provisions cover only the most minute part of the field, almost all court cases must be settled, as this one was, by reference to commercial practice.

[2] Mr. Justice Locke in the case of *Minister of National Revenue v. Anaconda American Brass Ltd.*, Supreme Court of Canada, November 1, 1954.

While financial statements were probably developed originally on a basis of legal concepts, it is tempting to conclude that the matter is now rather the other way around: statute requirements and legal decisions both follow changes in practice, rather than provide the basis for them. An interesting example is the preparation of consolidated statements for a group of companies. This is a recognition of the inadequacy, in actual business circumstances, of the legal concept of a corporation as a person. In preparing a consolidated statement, accountants are, in effect, looking through the strict legal situation to produce a set of statements that will adequately show the progress of a group of affiliated companies.

Statutory pronouncements and court decisions can therefore be expected to consolidate advances made in accounting—not to be the starting point for them.

There is danger in too great an emphasis on the legal elements in accounting. For example, there is some tendency to suggest that the only liabilities that should be set forth are those representing a legal obligation. Yet there are many liabilities a company will have to face, and that it should recognize if its balance sheet is to set forth its obligations fairly, that have no legal sanction at the balance sheet date.

An illustration of the misleading effect of too great an attention to legalities is in regard to "surplus." Legally the entire earned surplus of a corporation may be distributed in dividends, but it would be a mistake to conclude that this is actually a practical possibility in all cases. Theoretically, if there is no cash to pay dividends, money may be borrowed to pay them to the full amount of the stated surplus, but it is not hard to imagine situations in which this would be imprudent and even disastrous. In other words, the amount of surplus that can be legally paid out may be largely irrelevant. This prompts the question: If the surplus of a company, as established by statutory provisions, is not in fact available for dividends, is it correct to give the contrary impression by showing this amount as surplus in our financial statements?

Legislation is bound to be a clumsy and ineffective approach to statement reform. Such attempts as have been made to legislate for better disclosure have not always been very helpful. It is tempting to charge payments a company is not anxious to disclose to such non-committal sounding accounts as "promotion" or "legal expense" or "public relations." In the early days of company legislation it became popular to enact statutory requirements that the amounts charged to such accounts be specifically disclosed, but this was underestimating the alertness of corporation management. It was quite simple for the unscrupulous to think of another account to which dubious items could be charged, and it is of course only the unscrupulous who would want to hide such payments in the first place. The whole business of financial statement production is too complicated and imprecise for progress to be initiated by drafting specific statutory requirements.

The situation may be summed up by saying that in an increasingly complex business world, when better and better statements are needed, it would be wrong to stick with legal concepts which always must lag behind current requirements. The correct sequence in statement reform is: firstly, an experiment by a company wishing to establish itself as a leader; secondly, the formation of a consensus that the new development should be adopted; thirdly, perhaps confirmation by a pronouncement in court if the point comes up in a case; finally, embodiment in company law as a statutory requirement.

Confusion of means and ends

The fact that accountants normally spend much more time in preparing financial statements than in studying them has already been laboured. Absorption in the problem of statement preparation can encourage the development of a tendency, when a new problem arises, for accountants to rush to a consideration of the techniques by which the problem may be solved before establishing what the problem is.

Nothing illustrates this danger better than the confused discussions of recent years in regard to accounting for price level changes. There has been much good talk about how to cope with inflation in published accounts—but little action. Essentially this is because it is not yet too clear what the actual problem is. Is it to keep track of the general change in the value of currency in times of inflation? Or is it to assure the provision of funds to replace fixed assets? Or is it a matter of providing figures that will show a more useful calculation of profit? Until we are much clearer as to just what the problem is from the point of view of the statement user, a detailed discussion of techniques is a waste of time. Yet accountants are so much more at home in the field of accounting techniques than of statement interpretation, that there is a danger they may miss the significance of the problem by being prematurely absorbed in solutions. We can never expect to find the right answers until we are sure we know the right questions.

If the utility concept of accounting is indeed basically correct, accountants must clear their minds of a number of different types of error that lead to confusion and delay progress. Accountants really do not need to be particularly profound, but they must be more clear-headed.

6

Accounting for Special Purposes

To this point, an attempt has been made to establish the essential nature of financial reporting by working through a simple chain of reasoning. It is hoped that this has helped to clear away confusion and error so that our proper goals become apparent. We have concentrated on the published statements of commercial enterprises. This has left untouched several very important areas. There are, for example, the questions of taxable income and of management accounting, as well as the large subject of accounting for non-commercial enterprises. It is not intended to enter into any of these areas exhaustively because they are outside the main stream of our argument. They are, however, of tremendous importance and it is essential to consider each of them in relation to our theme.

A digression to these specialized types of accounting may serve to emphasize that accounting is not absolute in nature but rather that it is a practical art that needs to be adapted to several different purposes.

TAXABLE INCOME

The effect of adopting income as a tax base

Let us first consider taxable income. The adoption of income as a major base in our tax structures has had decisive effects on the development of accounting theory—both helpful and detrimental to progress. The development was helpful because it gave a new importance to income determination—and any problem that attracts serious attention tends to get solved. On the other hand, our severe income taxes also tend to complicate and hinder reformation—because each change is likely to raise the reported income of some taxpayers. Corporation executives thus often find themselves in a position where the immediate effect of acquiescing in a new method of income determination will be to increase taxes. As such executives are supposed to act in the best interests of the shareholders, the prospect of causing their company to pay more taxes is just one more reason to resist the adoption of new techniques; and this is a particularly unfortunate influence on a group that tend instinctively to be cautious enough about making changes in established procedures, at least in the financial field.

To examine first the favourable influence: the introduction of income taxes was one of the great turning points in the history of financial statements. Until the late nineteenth century, financial statements were prepared (as we have seen) largely for credit purposes. The balance sheet was all that counted. The income statement, if published at all, was considered a reconciliation of the change in net worth from one balance sheet date to the next.

With attention focused on credit, the only thing that mattered was that profit should not be overstated. With the increasing reliance on income taxes as a source of government revenue, two important new considerations arose. In the first place, a miscalculation of income, in addition to misleading some poor devil of an investor, could cost a company itself good hard cash. In this way an entirely new pressure was put on accurate income determination. In the second place, a serious group came into existence who had a direct interest and responsibility to see that income was not understated: the tax collectors, a team including both the responsible minister and the departmental staff. This was the group charged with designing a fair system and carrying out the assessing process. As tax rates tended to rise almost steadily in most countries, the influence of income tax determination on concepts of income became more and more decisive.

In this connection, it is interesting to reflect that in his *Principles of Political Economy* published just a hundred years ago, John Stuart Mill confessed his concern over what he described as "the great burden of taxes," which he felt might cripple the economy. No wonder he was worried, the income tax in England had just been raised again—this time from sixpence in the pound sterling to sevenpence. Currently the top rate is eighteen shillings and threepence in the pound. The increase since Mill's day has therefore been from 2½ per cent to over 90 per cent.

In the United States and Canada the corporation income tax rate has tended recently to hover around the 50 per cent level, and of course, heavy personal income taxes come on top of that. It is small wonder that the impact of income tax is a main thought in everyone's mind when an income statement is prepared. Any other attitude would be suicidal.

The determination of taxable income

It is the income tax collector's essential duty to establish a method of determining taxable income that will be as fair as possible to all taxpayers. As one would expect in any situation involving human beings, the most deeply cherished conviction of the tax collector is a strong faith in the taxpayer's ability to look after himself. Thus the collector's principal concern is likely to be to prevent income from being understated. In the last analysis, the collector should, however, be concerned with fair determination—and the law courts are there to see that he is.

In searching for the proper base for determining taxable income, legislatures and courts have, on the whole, adopted the approach that net income, as determined by generally accepted accounting principles, is the most appropriate concept. It is hard to argue against this for two compelling reasons. In the first place, this concept of net income has been developed by accountants from actual business experience as the best representation of income they can devise. In the second place, it is hard to imagine what other alternative there is. The tax departments are in no position to develop a different income concept of their own. If they seriously tried to do so, they would undoubtedly end up with some quite similar system, for the simple reason that the distillation of general rules from practice is about the only way anyone could go about the job.

While published net income was inescapably the general basis of income tax, there were certain areas—notably depreciation accounting—where special rules were found to be necessary from the start. It is interesting to observe the course of developments. To begin with, depreciation is at once a very important element in the operations of many companies and also the accounting area in which arbitrary rules have to have most play. This led, in the early days of income taxation, to the government stipulating maximum rates that would be allowable in determining taxable income. At first no great problem seemed to arise. Rates of tax were low, commercial life was relatively uncomplicated, and normally companies adopted the government maximum rates for their own accounting. Thus published net income and taxable income marched along pretty well in step.

Latterly this simple harmony has been disturbed, partly because of sharp increases in the tax rates and partly because governments have seized on the device of special depreciation allowances as a means of tax relief and of economic stimulation. The point has now been reached at which there are commonly wide differences between reported net income and taxable income. There are so many accelerated and special rates in effect that taxable income has begun to approach more nearly to cash flow than to net income. There is a certain logic to this. One of the important canons of taxation is ability to pay, and presumably taxes should be payable when cash is available. To follow this to a logical conclusion, income taxes should perhaps be turned into cash flow taxes.

The divergence of taxable income from reported net income has set the accounting profession one of its toughest problems: the satisfactory handling of deferred tax liabilities. Not without several false starts and not, indeed, without much blood, sweat, and tears, the profession has reached something fairly close to agreement on procedures for handling deferred tax liabilities. This being so, taxable income and reported net income will continue to approximate one another in the long run, in spite of year-by-year variations of considerable size.

No one should expect the tax collectors to be pioneers

As the tax collectors must, in the long run, follow generally accepted accounting principles, we have no right to expect them to be pioneers. They are not in any position to improve financial statements by inventing more useful forms of presentation. This is not their job. On the other hand, if experimentation in presentation leads to the adoption of improved accounting principles, eventually these have to be adopted for tax purposes.

Arguments between the taxpayer and the department are the essence of the whole income tax system. These are bound to result from a system under which the taxpayer is required to assess himself—and under which his assessment is then reviewed by the tax department. In the resulting arguments, attempts have sometimes been made to maintain that general accounting principles, while all very well for the production of financial statements, have no necessary application to the determination of taxable income. This sort of view is nonsensical. Short of some specific statutory provision (and such provisions can cover only a small part of the field), the tax department really have no alternative but to accept the principles that have been developed for producing general purpose statements in the business world. What other basis could there be?

The tax collectors' difficult job

To appreciate the position of the tax collectors, it must be understood that while the determination of income must always be a rough-and-ready business at best, at current high tax rates each variation in determining income is of vital importance. Assessing someone's taxable income is not an exercise in accounting theory, it involves deciding how much cash he must contribute to the state. Consider how this applies, say, to the vital distinction between capital expenditure and expense, which may be easy to draw in theory but which in actual practice presents many virtually insoluble problems. There are items that are clearly of a capital nature and other items that are clearly expenses; but between these clear-cut types of expenditure, there is a wide grey area where classification is arguable. If income tax was not such a tremendously important item—in other words, if tax rates were lower—it would be easier to reach agreement in distinguishing between items that should be capitalized and those that should be expensed. However, when the classification of an item as a capital expenditure costs a company a substantial amount in taxes, the analysis of grey items becomes an exceedingly tricky problem. Yet the tax assessor has no way of avoiding these difficult decisions: he must rule that each of the grey items is either black or white—either a deductible expense or not.

The true difficulty of the tax assessors' position can be fully appreciated only if we think of a wide range of transactions arranged in order: the strictly capital items placed on one side and the strictly expense items on the other, while between these extremes other mixed transactions are set out in order of the weight of the expense and capital elements in them. By this process a sort of continuous spectrum can be prepared running from black to white through every shade of grey. At some place the tax assessor must divide this range of transactions arbitrarily, and rule that a transaction on one side of the line is deductible for tax purposes, while a transaction on the other side is not deductible. He has no alternative; he must draw the line somewhere. Yet no matter where he draws it, it is bound to come between two almost indistinguishable neighbouring transactions that must thus be considered different for tax purposes. Under current tax rates, each difficult decision of this sort can cost a corporate taxpayer approximately 50 cents for every dollar involved in the transaction. It is a miracle that income tax can be made to work at all in these circumstances and great credit is due to all concerned: to the business men, to their accountants, and particularly to the tax assessors.

The pursuit of equity in taxation

If the government must collect a certain sum through income taxes (and this is an assumption we must accept), the important consideration for accountants is that this sum be collected as fairly as possible. Any change in the method of determining income should not affect the total amount collected by income taxes from all taxpayers, but should merely provide that the tax burden is spread as fairly as possible. Thus if new and better methods of income determination become accepted in business, the tax department has no reason to refuse to adopt them. If the new methods produce a fairer figure of income, they will, by the same token, provide a fairer base for taxable income.

Any change in accounting conventions is bound ultimately to increase income taxes for some taxpayers and reduce them for others. This is inevitable. It is quite natural that there should be a hesitancy to support a reform in financial presentation that will cost additional income tax. However, if financial statements are to be improved, the overall effect will not be to increase tax payments, but simply to spread them more fairly. It is thus in the long-range interest of companies to encourage the production of a fairer income figure, even though this may involve some increase in their current tax bill. To argue otherwise is to suggest that no change in financial statements can ever be implemented. In the long run this might prove very expensive.

We should not ask the tax authorities to be experimenters and innovators in financial presentation. However, if we can develop the general acceptance of better methods of income determination, we have every right to expect the tax authorities to adhere to these methods once they are generally accepted. Thus while changes in presentation may not have any immediate bearing on the determination of taxable income, eventually they should have such effect, to the general benefit of all taxpayers, because the fairer the method of determining taxable income the better for everyone.

It might be reiterated that taxpayers are going to have to develop a sophisticated view of income determination. If they insist on opposing any change that will result in an increase in their current taxable income, they must accept the indefinite continuation of all the inequities built into our present tax system by unsound principles.

MANAGEMENT ACCOUNTING

Reporting for different types of businesses

In respect to their accounting requirements, businesses can be divided into three classes:

1. There are very small businesses that require no financial statements at all. These can be run under the personal observation of the owner. A peanut stand would

illustrate this sort of business. Even somewhat more elaborate ventures can sometimes be reasonably well managed with virtually no paper work at all.

2. Larger concerns need some statements, but can get by reasonably well with only general purpose statements.
3. In very large public companies, management requires an entirely different type of statement—more detailed and more specialized.

It has already been explained that the specialized statements required for management purposes in large businesses are not the subject of this present study. However, such statements are of great importance and a few paragraphs must be devoted to them.

Large companies needing sophisticated information have sometimes considered themselves bound, in the production of their internal management statements, by the sort of generally accepted accounting principles that have been developed to produce general purpose statements. There is really no need for the internal statements to be restricted in this way. It is in fact important to free the accountant from any unnecessary restrictions in producing management statements; and it should be recognized that management is entitled to any form of statement that would be helpful in running the business.

To insist on adherence to generally accepted accounting principles where they do not apply is obviously wrongheaded. For example, in the early days of cost accounting, it was accepted as necessary that the detailed cost accounts should tie in and be reconcilable with the regular annual financial statements prepared for shareholders. In fact, early texts on cost accounting implied that this was the most important feature in a properly designed cost system. There was, of course, some point in this insistence on a tie-in of costs with published statements. It was intended as a useful control over the accuracy and realism of cost calculations. However, this insistence on a reconciliation with the shareholders' statements diverted attention from the really basic purpose of a cost system: the provision of data to management that is useful in making business decisions. It was almost as though the accountant considered the essential purpose of cost accounting the dividing up of the total company expenses over its products. In making the necessary allocations to do this, essentially arbitrary and irrelevant pro-rations had to be made, and management must have been misled frequently by the resulting "costs."

A broad overall picture is not the goal in management accounting. The goal is significant detailed reports on different aspects of a corporation's activities. The main object is to sort out, in so far as this is feasible, the results of the activities of different departments or cost centres so that the effectiveness of each group's operation can be judged. There are no universal rules to apply here. The only criterion is what figures should be produced to provide the best control over the different operations of the company.

Management accounting and custodial accounting

It is now increasingly recognized that management accounting is and should be quite different from what is sometimes referred to as "custodial accounting."

In a recent text, the relationship between the different kinds of accounting required by large modern corporations is defined in the following terms:

> All of the business accounting functions can be classified into three major conceptual categories which have significantly different objectives. Although the following classification may at first seem rather pointless from an accounting viewpoint, it is quite useful for focusing attention on the different objectives of the accounting

system. It distinguishes among decisions as to what plans the business should adopt, measurement of detailed performance against these plans, and the over-all financial results of this performance.

Custodial accounting is defined as the financial acounting for the assets entrusted to the enterprise. It is basically concerned with preparation of reports and data for groups or persons other than management. This includes the preparation and presentation of reports to stockholders, as well as to creditors or governmental agencies such as the SEC or the Internal Revenue Service.

Performance accounting is the quantitative matching of performance against some plan by organizational responsibility. It includes all accounting procedures and reports which exist in order to evaluate organizational performance. Performance accounting includes the functions which some accountants call responsibility accounting, i.e., the collection of costs by organizational responsibility. It also deals, however, with quantitative data other than costs. This may include such things as product line revenue, physical workload statistics, and internal net income reports. It implies the use of standards and budgets. Its distinguishing characteristic is that it serves to measure actual performance against planned performance by responsibility.

Decision accounting is the quantitative evaluation of alternative courses of action. It includes all disciplined techniques for providing quantitative information in the form which can best assist a specific management decision at the time when the decision has to be made. This includes all of the profit planning decisions as to product pricing, make or buy, inventory policies, and choice of alternative production methods. It is the area in which business has historically depended on special analyses and memorandum accounts.

The last two of the above classes are grouped in the minds of many under the heading of "managerial accounting.". . .[1]

Custodial accounting must, as we have insisted, be based on generally accepted accounting principles. Its main function, as the name implies, is to provide a report on stewardship. Are the assets being carefully looked after? Is the

[1] Robert Beyer, C.P.A., *Profitability Accounting for Planning and Control* (New York: The Ronald Press Co., 1963), pp.16–17.

company maintaining a solvent position? Is it progressing satisfactorily in regard to profits? These are the sort of questions the custodial statements are intended to answer. Management is basically interested in these questions too but, in large corporations, requires much more detailed information, and often quite a different sort of information.

The function of the accountant is to provide those who need information with statements that will be useful to them. He is responsible for keeping the records from which the statements are prepared and for providing control over all transactions. The records in his care must be kept up-to-date and information must be available promptly. It is also the accountant's responsibility to indicate to management the different types of statements that can be produced. Beyond this point, it becomes management's job—and not the accountant's job—to decide what sort of statements should be produced.

The production of satisfactory statements for management, in today's conditions of increasing complexity, has become the chief accounting problem in large corporations and is entitled to first priority over all other accounting requirements. The accounting system should be basically designed to produce the information that management needs. Custodial accounting, however important, comes after management accounting. The accountant must think first of the requirements of good statements for management. Once these have been produced, it is a relatively simple matter to make the necessary adjustments to produce satisfactory custodial statements.

Cost accounting

Cost accounting is largely designed for management purposes: to form a basis for production or purchase programs, to establish proper prices, to trace down profits to individual lines, and so on. It has some relevance for custodial purposes, such as providing a basis for proper inventory valuation. However, there are many different types of cost accounting and the cost system should be basically directed to giving management the information it needs.

ACCOUNTING OUTSIDE THE BUSINESS WORLD

Many interesting and instructive accounting problems are encountered in attempting to produce the financial reports of non-profit-making organizations. These problems are not treated in this book as such organizations are not faced with the toughest of all accounting problems: the determination of periodic net income. This fact is somewhat concealed because churches, clubs, school boards, trade unions, and the great variety of other non-commercial groups do usually attempt to produce statements in the conventional commercial pattern of balance sheet and income statement. The statements of all such groups thus tend to be derivative. They are based on commercial practice lightly adapted to their special needs.

It might be pointed out in passing that the main mistake in non-commercial accounting has been a tendency to follow too closely rules developed in the commercial world and quite inappropriate elsewhere. For the light it throws on the nature of financial reporting, consider the tricky case presented by statements for social clubs. As anyone who has ever had anything to do with trying to run such clubs soon learns, the only accounting principle of any validity in these cases is that one must not report an excess of revenue over expenditure—however microscopic. To do so simply invites members to clamour for a reduction of fees. Yet through some notion that it is "businesslike" (in the favourable sense of that term), it is common for such clubs to adopt the whole paraphernalia of commercial practice, including accrual and depreciation accounting. The result is that we arrive at an excess of revenue over expenditure (or vice versa) that has no significance to anyone.

The relation between revenue and expenditure is important in a commercial venture, because it may indicate whether the operation is going to survive and flourish or not. In a private club, this relationship between revenue and expenditure, as calculated on pseudo-commercial principles, may not mean anything at all. In the typical case, club members should be concerned about just two things:

1. Are current revenue and expenditure in such balance that the club can meet its current operating obligations?
2. Are there any large capital obligations hanging over the membership (such as the replacement of the club house)?

It is most unlikely that commercial-style depreciation accounting will present these two basic aspects of a club's operations in the clearest possible way. And this point has been laboured because great confusion in accounting thought has resulted from the uncritical assumption that what is a sound accounting rule for one organization will necessarily be a good rule for all others. This we might describe as the Bullmoose fallacy: "What's good for General Bullmoose is good for everybody."

To make this elementary but basic point clear: The annual statement of The Downtown Club might look something like this if kept in the usual manner with commercial style depreciation:

Assets:		
Cash	$ 2,000	
Receivables	32,000	
Inventories	1,000	$ 35,000
Property	200,000	
Less: Depreciation	120,000	80,000
		$115,000

Liabilities:		
Current payables		$ 18,000
Mortgage payable		60,000
Members' equity:		
At start	46,000	
Less: Excess expenditure for period	9,000	37,000
		$115,000

Revenue:		
Fees	20,000	
Dining and bar	35,000	$ 55,000
Expenditure:		
Expenses	54,000	
Depreciation	10,000	64,000
Excess expenditure		$ 9,000

The only information this form of presentation provides is the almost unconcealable fact that the working capital position is satisfactory. No conclusion can be drawn from the excess expenditure, even though this is large for this size of operation. Moreover, to present the finances of the club in this form invites the drawing of quite misleading conclusions. It might suggest that the financial position of the club is deteriorating and that fees must be raised, but this only follows if the value of the property has deteriorated or some large rebuilding program will be necessary in the relatively near future.

Surely this would be clearer if the management discarded inapplicable commercial forms and presented the financial position in some such form as this:

Operations:

Expenses	$54,000
Less: Dining and bar revenue	35,000
Loss on operations	19,000
Fees	20,000
Increase in working capital	$ 1,000

Working Capital:

	Start	*Close*	*Change*
Cash	$ 1,000	$ 2,000	$ 1,000
Receivables	29,000	32,000	3,000
Inventories	1,000	1,000	–
	31,000	35,000	
Payables	15,000	18,000	(3,000)
	$16,000	$17,000	$ 1,000

Property:

The club has invested $200,000 in property, principally in the club house which was built in 1950 and is in excellent repair. No major expenditure on the property is under contemplation. The property is mortgaged for $60,000.

The foregoing presentation is designed on the principle that the basic concern of club members is solvency. It would seem reasonable to conclude that operations are satisfactory on the basis of these figures. On the other hand, had a major investment in properties been contemplated, presumably some plan for financing the investment would be presented—such as a proposal to increase fees, get more members, or borrow.

Similarly, statements for hospitals, churches, government commissions, and so on should be designed to suit the particular requirements of each type of operation. Generally accepted accounting principles should be used where appropriate, but it should not be assumed that such principles will necessarily apply.

A final illustration of the unsuitability of a routine commercial approach to institutional statements might be provided by a consideration of the financial statements of universities.

Normally universities produce balance sheets and income statements in conventional pattern. The income statement concludes with a figure described as the "Excess of Income over Expenditure"—or more commonly the reverse. What does such a figure really mean? It might be assumed that a black figure signified a satisfactory position and a red figure an unsatisfactory one. But this would be quite erroneous, as can be appreciated by a consideration of the facts of life in university administration.

The expenditure budget of a university does not represent the amount it should spend. There would be no way of arriving at such a figure. There is not a university in existence anywhere that could not legitimately, and without extravagance, spend at least 50 per cent more than it is budgeting to spend without enrolling any more students. Excellence in education means the best teachers, the best library and laboratory facilities, and a low student-staff ratio. Without wall-to-wall carpeting and other luxuries, an almost limitless amount could be usefully spent to improve the quality of the education provided. Because in higher education at least, while spending money does not necessarily mean high quality, it is undoubtedly true that high quality means spending money.

The job facing university authorities in preparing a budget is to gather together an estimate of what they would like to spend and what they have any hope of collecting—and universities being what they are, the former always greatly exceeds the latter. As a balanced budget must be aimed at in the pursuit of survival, proposed expenditures must be cut back until there is some hope of meeting them by the amounts anticipated from grants, donations, fees, and other available sources.

It is not the objective of a university to give the best possible education regardless of cost. It is easy to imagine where such a policy would lead. The real objective of a university should be to collect as much as it can from all sources available to it, and to spend this money as wisely as possible so that the students entrusted to its care will get the best possible education with the funds available.

With this background, it can be appreciated that an excess of revenue over expenditure in a university's statement does not indicate a surplus. It simply means that the university has not spent as much as it should have spent, owing to the inherent vagaries of estimating revenue. This would not be guessed from a statement showing excess revenue, which implies that the university has been getting more money than it needs. Surely some different form of statement could be devised that would not be so likely to be misleading on the one most crucial fact in the university's financial position.

We can observe from these brief excursions into non-commercial accounting that financial statements in this area are subject to the same basic rule that they should be designed to provide the most useful information procurable.

This cavalier treatment of non-commercial accounting should not suggest that it is unimportant, but merely that it must develop along quite different lines from commercial accounting; and we choose the latter as the theme of this book because it is the more highly developed and controversial field.

With these digressions into the neighbouring fields of tax, management, and non-profit accounting behind us, we return in the next chapters to a consideration of the steps that should be taken to improve the quality of conventional commercial statements.

7

The Unending Search for Clarity of Presentation

THE POET WORDSWORTH used to worry his sister Dorothy by spending days groping gravely for a felicitous turn to a single phrase, to the visible impairment of his health. In a way, this is the lot of anyone in the business of communicating ideas, be he poet or accountant. We can never be satisfied with our current performance. But improving financial statements cannot be regarded as a sort of pursuit of the Holy Grail—disinterested, sublime, and contemptuous of the inconvenient facts of life. It is not only important that we produce better statements but very urgent that we do so quickly.

To this juncture, we have been pointing out some of the things that are wrong with our statements. This is a congenial role for an accountant. He tends to be much more at home in insisting on what is wrong than in doing something practical to put it right. However, we must face up to the problem of suggesting how better statements can actually be produced.

We must heed the advice, said to have been given to one of his junior Cabinet Ministers, by Sir Winston Churchill in the darkest hours of the War, when the fate of the world seemed to hang in the balance. The Minister (or so the story goes) had become involved in a battle with the Press on some issue quite irrelevant to the basic problem of national survival, and had submitted a lengthy account of the situation with a detailed defence of his point of view. In reply Sir Winston said merely that he would be obliged if the Minister would attempt to overcome his difficulties instead of entrenching himself behind them.

We must rush out from behind the barricades to the attack, however dangerous this may be. This will involve abandoning two attitudes fatal to progress. One is fear of change on the general grounds that it is always possible we may get into an even worse mess than we are in now. The other is a fear that presenting the facts more clearly and realistically may have painful consequences. For example, if profits are really higher than disclosed by current accounting conventions, to state them properly might lead to higher taxes or a clamour for increased dividends or some other development uncongenial to management. If these attitudes are to be allowed to persist, it is ridiculous to attempt to produce better statements. We might as well stop trying to.

The case for accounting reform is, of course, not based on the idea that management should be urged to commit hari-kari by accepting a type of statement that will run their corporations into bankruptcy. The case for reform is that, in the long run, fair disclosure is in the interest of everyone, and that our complex economy will operate most efficiently if there are statements available to management, investors, and all other interested parties that explain rather than conceal what is going on. The first step in developing better statements is to want to produce them.

Accounting research

One essential of progress is effective research. Now "research" is very much an okay word these days, with its exciting flavour of space-age living. Like other popular terms, however, it is perhaps somewhat overused, being applied to a variety of quite different projects. In fact, in accounting, "research" has come to mean almost anything written on the subject.

We need to start by distinguishing between two broad research fields. There is what might be called fundamental research. This is the probing of our accounting concepts in depth in an attempt to roll back the frontiers of accounting knowledge. This sort of thing should be mainly the concern of our academics and our institutes. It is essential work. If in this present text it appears to have been somewhat played down, this is because a great deal of first-class work is going on in this area—so much so that we are here well ahead of the progress in the other important research area: the applied research required to develop practical applications of what we already do know. There has been much more good talking and good writing than progress in applying the new ideas thus generated.

We are somewhat in the position of the farmer who wrote to the Department of Agriculture saying: "Please stop sending me those booklets telling me how to farm better—I ain't farming as good as I know how right now."

These two types of research require exactly contrary points of view. In fundamental research into concepts, the struggle is always to find the ideal answer. We live in the kind of world where the ideal does not get attained, but it must always be the goal. On the other hand, in applied research ideals have no place. The objective in applied research is not to wait for the ideal solution, which will never come, but to make some progress by putting to use what we do already know, imperfect though it be. What we are looking for is not an ideal statement but simply for something better than we have. It is the domain of the comparative rather than the superlative.

The field of applied accounting research has this in common with fundamental research: the search is unending there too. It is inconceivable that financial statements could ever be produced that were not susceptible to improvement. Even if statements could be produced that were completely satisfactory, changing economic circumstances would create new problems; and different and still better statements would again be required.

To say that the statements we produce are just not good enough is not to deride the efforts of the past. Derision would be quite out of place. Financial statements, as now produced, are the result of many years of patient striving for clearer presentation. On the other hand, if derision is out of place, so is reverence. We must stand back in detachment and weigh modern financial statements coolly and objectively.

The age of change

It should be quite evident that accounting problems are enormously accentuated by the fact that we live in an era of breathless change—with most of the changes in the direction of increasing size and complexity. It would be relatively easy to develop satisfactory statements in a static economy. In the process of time we might expect new procedures to evolve that would eventually lead to a completely satisfactory type of statement. But this is not the situation.

We live in a sort of Through-the-Looking-Glass world, where we must run very fast just to stay in the same place. It is hard to imagine a slowing down of the tempo of change. The probability is surely that the tempo will accelerate rather than slow down.

The effect of all such changes must be fully appreciated to grasp the fundamental crisis in accounting today. It would be bad enough if we simply had to close the gap between the kind of statements that are needed and the kind that are being produced, but the situation is worse than this. We must also develop some technique for improving statements that will enable us to keep up with the more and more demanding requirements that are certain to emerge from the current trends toward complexity in business.

Better special purpose statements

There is of course a constant challenge to produce improved financial statements for all sorts of special purposes, but this is not a problem that need concern us here. Moreover, it is relatively straightforward. We need simply remember that in producing special purpose statements we are free of the limitations of general acceptance, and can concentrate on the specific needs and requirements of those for whom the statements are prepared. The problem is to find out what the user really wants and to reconcile this, as best the accountant may, with what can be provided.

Better general purpose statements

When we move from special purpose to general purpose statements, we encounter an entirely new situation. We have seen that general purpose statements must meet a variety of needs, and that they must be understandable to "outsiders." This means they must be prepared on an agreed and recognized basis. Once a statement ceases to be directed specifically to a certain purpose, it has to have a sort of intrinsic validity in its own right. It must prove useful to anyone who wants to find out about the resources and operating results of the company. It must, as it were, stand on its own feet. Thus, as soon as one has to deal with general purpose statements, one has to face the concept of generally accepted principles.

As we have already insisted, there is no right or wrong way of producing financial information; there are simply more useful and less useful presentations. There is no true presentation or false; there are merely ways that are appropriate for certain purposes and ways appropriate for others. If there are no absolute values, there are, of course, relative values. Some statements now being issued are better than others. When we seek to base our principles on practice, we must, of course, select the better statements rather than the poorer; and this introduces problems too because individuals can disagree in some cases as to which form of presentation is preferable. Fortunately a reasonable consensus has usually been reached—not unanimity always, but a fair consensus.

When we say, then, that our general principles should be based on procedures from the actual business world, we mean on procedures that a consensus of those knowledgeable in the field would consider to be the best in use.

We inevitably must come back to the position that accounting can only be based on general acceptance. There is no practical alternative. Metaphysical approaches are too vague and legal provisions too specific. We will undoubtedly continue to get some help from the techniques developed in the sciences, and we may expect some day that accounting will come quite close, in its procedures, to some of the sciences; but all this is distant. For the present we must continue to rely chiefly on practical rules developed in the running of businesses.

The stark dilemma of the accountant can only be fully appreciated in all its perplexity by setting side by side the two inescapable conclusions just discussed:

1. There are constant changes in the sort of statements required.
2. The only practicable basis on which useful statements can be produced is general acceptance.

How can better (and therefore, by definition, different) statements be produced if the basis on which statements are produced must be sanctioned by general acceptance? This is the sort of dilemma that leads even the most sensible of accounting bodies to get manoeuvred into making pronouncements such as that contained in *Bulletin No. 11* of the Committee on Accounting and Auditing Research of The Canadian Institute of Chartered Accountants:

> Unless replacement cost accounting becomes generally acceptable, the writing up of fixed asset values should not occur and should be discouraged.[1]

The implication is presumably that if, in spite of discouragement from the accounting profession, such write-ups nevertheless become accepted, the basis of current statements should be changed. Not a very helpful attitude.

[1] August, 1955.

The general acceptance of more useful principles

The goal in the crusade for better financial statements therefore inescapably resolves itself into providing techniques for getting agreement to better (more useful) principles.

One obvious way to effect such agreement would be to summon a conference of experts, who would study various suggestions and recommend useful changes. One way or another, a good deal of this sort of thing goes on, and it does help solve some problems. However, no matter how much we encourage this sort of theoretical approach, it will never provide the whole answer. In fact the only area in which such gatherings of experts can be expected to help is in fundamental research into concepts. As has been suggested already, this is essentially the responsibility of the universities and the professional institutes.

The most valuable theoretical discussions amongst experts has perhaps been provided by the deliberations of the research committees of our accounting institutes. These committees have many characteristics that help them in coming to agreement. They represent a carefully selected cross-section of the accounting profession. There are no troublesome economists present to confuse the issues. The committees are kept down to a relatively small and manageable size. Yet with all these advantages, the research committees in their pronouncements have had to keep to relatively uncontroversial grounds, in order to gain general acceptance. In the result, these research committees have tended to stay well behind the best current practice and have usually made pronouncements only in areas of least controversy. Where they have ventured into the realm of controversy, the results have not been happy. It would seem that such committees can hope only to codify well-accepted practice rather than lead in introducing new improvements. If, with all the advantages they have, such committees cannot break new ground effectively, other groups, with wider representation, can still less hope to do so.

There is the further difficulty that, if our thesis is correct that better financial statements will only come if the requirements of users are reconciled with the feasibilities of production, it would seem to follow that pronouncements to have proper weight should represent the views of both users and producers. A good cross-section of accountants is not enough. To widen the representation however would still further limit the areas where agreement could be expected from theoretical discussion.

We can sum up this part of the problem by concluding that, no matter how we judge the progress now being made in discussions among experts, and no matter how much better we hope to do in this respect in the future, we might as well face squarely up to the fact that we are not going to solve our reporting problems by this means.

The need for experiment

What we come up flatly against is the inescapable proposition that we are not going to progress much faster unless someone starts actually publishing better statements. Clearly we must encourage companies to experiment and to make use of more of the good research already available.

If fundamental research is peculiarly the responsibility of the universities and the institutes, as has been suggested, surely the applied research that goes into the production of statements is the inescapable responsibility of the companies that publish the statements. These companies are well supplied with professional accountants on their own staffs and as auditors and consultants. Plenty of ideas have been batted around. It is time to find out which of them would prove serviceable in practice.

To embark on a policy of vigorous encouragement to experiment would require a complete change of heart by everyone concerned. At present all the pressure is in the opposite direction. Public companies, though they have become much more communicative than they used to be, still tend to be cautious in providing financial information to outsiders. Accountants have the inbred caution that comes with their heavy responsibility for the supportability of their statements. Perhaps more serious still has been the influence of regulatory bodies. These bodies are characteristically on the outlook for skullduggery, which makes them inclined to view with suspicion any unusual form of presentation. The weighty influence of all three of these groups tends therefore to be on the side of established practice and against innovation.

The essential factor of comparability

When we talk of experimentation and the encouragement of change, we must not forget the essential importance of comparability in financial statements. The basic techniques in statement analysis rely heavily on comparisons. Any set of statements means less by itself than when compared with other statements: those of the same company for other periods or those of competing companies for the same period.

From the point of view of comparability, the more uniformity the better; and this might seems to suggest the discouraging of experiments by individual companies. Indeed, comparability is so essential that it must be protected in any program of experimentation. Fortunately, this is not too difficult to provide for. It is always possible through supplementary information to give the details necessary for a serious analyst (the only kind we need worry about) to recast the statements on a conventional basis. Such data can usually be included in statement footnotes.

No analyst can then claim he has lost anything by being presented with a statement that departs in some respect from generally accepted principles. If he does not agree that the information on the new basis is more useful, he has the means of converting to the old. And, of course, another simple method of dealing with the problem is for the company to recast the statement itself and issue both the conventional form and what it considers a new improved form.

More experimenting would be most stimulating. Each company could learn from the efforts of others. If a certain experiment in presentation proved useful, it would be copied. If someone else produced an even better method, the previous experiment would be superseded. This would not change in any way the fundamentally necessary principle that accounting is based on a consensus of the well-informed. It would simply provide a means of speeding up the process of changing the consensus to keep it up-to-date.

There would be a still more important benefit from more innovation. We would discover the real problems of statement presentation instead of simply listening to accountants pontificating on what they suppose the problems might be. As in so many other realms, the old maxim holds true that you never know until you have tried. The real impact of this can be appreciated only by someone who has discussed an accounting proposal exhaustively in a group of experts and has then tried to put it into practice. The problems the experts anticipate often have little resemblance to the problems actually encountered in implementation. Sometimes a point that gives rise to great argument, and that appears almost insoluble, will prove relatively easy to work out in practice. On the other hand, it is quite probable that many tough problems will arise in practice that even the most alert of experts will have failed to foresee.

Thus any attempt to produce a new type of statement, or a statement with some new feature, is almost sure to advance accounting thinking.

The Imperial Tobacco case

There have of course been companies who have ventured out bravely with new forms of presentation; the trouble is that there simply have not been enough of them.

An interesting case study is provided by the Imperial Tobacco Company of Canada, Limited which produced its statements for the year 1961 on a basis of valuing its fixed assets at current costs. Companies had of course sometimes had their fixed assets appraised and had had such appraised values incorporated in their accounts. What was novel in this case was that the company announced a policy of adjusting the value of its assets systematically each year; and it was typical of the spirit in which the change was made that the company made no claim to having found the ultimate answer to fixed asset valuation. It simply announced that it considered the new presentation more significant than the old, and intended to go on using it until someone thought of a still better way.

The write-up of fixed asset values required, of course, an adjustment to accumulated depreciation and provided a new basis for calculating the annual depreciation charge. A footnote indicated the original cost of the fixed assets and the annual charge for depreciation on the old cost basis. By a couple of simple additions and deductions, an analyst could therefore reproduce the statements on conventional lines if he preferred them that way.

In the process of preparing the statements in new form, the company encountered all sorts of difficulties—most of which were not referred to in the copious literature on asset valuation, and few of which were mentioned amongst the difficulties the experts expected to encounter in undertaking a revaluation. None of these difficulties proved insuperable, although some were inevitably solved less satisfactorily than others. The final result was good, and stood up to the scrutiny of the financial community. The company has continued since to use this form of presentation.

Solutions in practice

To illustrate how much easier it is to solve problems when you settle down and tackle them rather than confine yourself to sitting around arguing about them in theory, consider the problem encountered by Imperial Tobacco in regard to the treatment of the appraisal surplus or credit that arose from the write-up of the assets.

In establishing current values for fixed assets, the company used appraisals by outside experts and index numbers applied to cost, according to which method seemed appropriate to the type of asset being dealt with. It was easily established that certain index numbers were appropriate to some types of equipment and different ones to others. However, a satisfactory current value for fixed assets emerged eventually, and it was difficult for anyone to claim that original cost represented a more useful valuation.

It was important to adjust accumulated depreciation so that this would be on the same basis as the asset valuation. It was intended to make the annual depreciation charge on this basis too, and in fact, the main purpose of the revaluation was to establish a more realistic annual charge. A most interesting point arose when the adjustment of accumulated depreciation was tackled. It was of course clear that this problem would recur each year in which there was any change in the asset valuation.

When the amount of depreciation required on the new basis was established, it had to be decided whether the additional requirement should be provided by a charge against retained earnings or by a charge against the capital increment arising from revaluation. As any two accountants can prove to themselves by getting into a discussion on the subject, this is an almost insoluble problem in theory. An excellent case can be made for each of the alternative treatments.

The effect of making adjustments to accumulated depreciation through retained earnings is that capital increment continues to be carried at the full difference between current values and original cost; whereas if adjustments to accumulated depreciation are made through capital increment, the latter represents the net effect of all adjustments.

In the Imperial Tobacco case this particular point led to lively debate, and eventually those working on the statements tended to be divided between the "gross" and "net" schools of thought. A decision was finally reached quite simply by calling a halt to argument and working out examples of the picture each method would produce in practice. When this was done, it became apparent that the "gross" method was much the better.

In the table on pages 138–39 two illustrations are submitted of how these methods work out by considering fixed assets costing $100,000 that have an estimated useful life of twenty years and are amortized at 5 per cent straight-line. Example A assumes fairly steady inflation and stable but gradually rising earnings (which represents a quite probable expectation). Example B assumes violent fluctuations in values and earnings. This table is worth a bit of study.

Point 1. It might first be observed that both these methods result in accumulating at the end of the asset's estimated useful life $154,000. This is the estimated current cost of replacing it. The logic of this has been widely questioned on the grounds that in practice fixed assets are rarely replaced, because of technological change. There is considerable force in this argument if the word "replacement" is taken literally. However, where possible, replacement should be not literally the cost of an identical asset, but the current cost of an asset of equal capacity. In buildings, for example, the replacement cost of a sixty-year-old factory should not be considered as the cost of reproducing some Edwardian monstrosity in granite—something no one would dream of doing and probably could not do if one tried. The current value should be taken as the cost of a modern building of the same capacity.

Point 2. For an accounting method to be acceptable, it should function satisfactorily under all conditions: inflation and deflation, profits and losses, relative stability and violent fluctuations.

In the two simple examples given in the table, the way the method works out is much more readily seen from Example B which deals with violent fluctuations. Under stable conditions the effects are not so obvious but they may be demonstrated to follow essentially the same pattern.

Assumptions:
Cost: $100,000
Useful life: 20 years
Depreciation at 5% straight-line
At end of tenth year decision made to revalue fixed asset at current values each year
Retained earnings at end of tenth year: $80,000

Year	Asset Value	Depreciation: Annual Charge	Transfer *	Accumulated
	Example A			
10 Original	$100,000			$ 50,000
10 Revised	130,000		$15,000	65,000
11	131,000	$ 6,550	500	72,050
12	133,000	6,650	1,100	79,800
13	135,000	6,750	1,200	87,750
14	140,000	7,000	3,250	98,000
15	144,000	7,200	2,800	108,000
16	146,000	7,300	1,500	116,800
17	150,000	7,500	3,200	127,500
18	151,000	7,550	850	135,900
19	151,000	7,550		143,450
20	154,000	7,700	2,850	154,000
		$71,750	$32,250	
	Example B			
10 Original	$100,000			$ 50,000
10 Revised	130,000		$15,000	65,000
11	135,000	$ 6,750	1,500	73,250
12	142,000	7,100	4,850	85,200
13	150,000	7,500	4,800	97,500
14	145,000	7,250	(3,250)	101,500
15	148,000	7,400	2,100	111,000
16	120,000	6,000	(21,000)	96,000
17	100,000	5,000	(16,000)	85,000
18	80,000	4,000	(17,000)	72,000
19	90,000	4,500	9,000	85,500
20	154,000	7,700	60,800	154,000
		$63,200	$40,800	

* The transfer to (or from) accumulated depreciation is to "Retained Earn-

Fixed Asset Depreciation Examples

Example A assumes fairly steady inflation and stable but gradually rising earnings.

Example B assumes quite violent fluctuations in values and earnings.

Net Asset Value	Annual Earnings	"Gross" Basis Retained Earnings	"Gross" Basis Capital Increment	"Net" Basis Retained Earnings	"Net" Basis Capital Increment
$50,000		$ 80,000		$ 80,000	
65,000		65,000	$30,000	80,000	$15,000
58,950	$ 12,000	76,500	31,000	92,000	15,500
53,200	14,000	89,400	33,000	106,000	16,400
47,250	18,000	106,200	35,000	124,000	17,200
42,000	14,000	116,950	40,000	138,000	18,950
36,000	16,000	130,150	44,000	154,000	20,150
29,200	20,000	148,650	46,000	174,000	20,650
22,500	20,000	165,450	50,000	194,000	21,450
15,100	23,000	187,600	51,000	217,000	21,600
7,550	30,000	217,600	51,000	247,000	21,600
	26,000	240,750	54,000	273,000	21,750
	$193,000				
$50,000		$ 80,000		$ 80,000	
65,000		65,000	$30,000	80,000	$15,000
61,750	$ 12,000	75,500	35,000	92,000	18,500
56,800	18,000	88,650	42,000	110,000	20,650
52,500	14,000	97,850	50,000	124,000	23,850
43,500	8,000	109,100	45,000	132,000	22,100
37,000	(6,000)	101,000	48,000	126,000	23,000
24,000	(20,000)	102,000	20,000	106,000	16,000
15,000	15,000	133,000		121,000	12,000
8,000	3,000	153,000	(20,000)	124,000	9,000
4,500	(10,000)	134,000	(10,000)	114,000	10,000
	15,000	88,200	54,000	129,000	13,200
	$ 49,000				

ings" on the " 'Gross' Basis," and to "Capital Increment" on the " 'Net' Basis."

Point 3. Illustrations of various treatments may be worked out by taking the figures from Example B and assuming the company originated in year 1 by the issue of $150,000 of common stock.

The balance sheet at year 20 would appear as follows under conventional accounting rules:

Assets:		
Fixed at cost	$100,000	
Less: Depreciation	100,000	–
Other assets (net)		$292,200
		$292,200
Net worth:		
Capital		$150,000
Retained earnings:		
Years 1–10	$ 80,000	
Years 11–20	49,000	
Depreciation added back	13,200	142,200
		$292,200

This form of presentation suggests that $142,200 could be paid out in dividends, but if this had been done the company would not be able to stay in business by purchasing fixed assets of equivalent capacity without raising additional capital or borrowing.

In practice, companies tend to pay out less than their full earnings in the pursuit of prudence. But there is nothing in this form of statement to indicate what part of the accumulated earnings it is prudent to retain.

Point 4. With current value accounting under both "gross" and "net" methods, the asset side of the balance sheet at year 20 would show:

Fixed assets at current value	$154,000	
Less: Depreciation	154,000	–
Other assets (net)		$292,200
		$292,200

Under the "gross" method the net worth would be:

Capital		$150,000
Retained earnings	$ 88,200	
Capital increment	54,000	142,200
		$292,200

While under the "net" method the corresponding figures would be:

Capital		$150,000
Retained earnings	$129,000	
Capital increment	13,200	142,200
		$292,200

The choice between these two methods is not based on theoretical considerations but simply on the practical question of which provides the more useful picture.

The advantage seems clearly in favour of the gross method. Under that method, $54,000 represents the amount of earnings it is estimated the company should retain to stay in its present business without additional financing; and therefore $88,200 represents an estimate of the earnings that might be distributed. In a practical case, other matters of prudence would enter, but its remains true that this presentation copes with one of the essential factors: the maintenance of the fixed assets required to keep the operation going.

It can of course be argued that the basic figure of $154,000 is only an estimate—subject to error and all sorts of qualifications. But the argument is not that this valuation is unassailable; the argument is merely that it represents information far more likely to be useful than the original cost of the asset twenty years previously.

In contrast, the picture presented by the net method is considerably less significant. The capital increment balance of $13,200 represents simply the difference between the increased value of the asset ($54,000) and the net amount of the annual adjustments to accumulated depreciation ($40,800). This is not a figure of importance to anyone.

Moreover, looking over the whole period, it will be observed that the gross method always shows the difference between the current value and original cost as a capital increment; while the net method produces erratic results. For example, at year 18 when the value of the asset has dropped $20,000 below cost, the net method still shows a capital increment of $9,000—a result contrary to common sense.

As a final point, it might be observed that while all three of these presentations naturally indicate the same increase in net worth ($142,200) at year 20, when the asset is completely written off, this would not be true in the intervening years 2 to 19.

Point 5. From the important aspect of comparisons with other companies, the earnings of this company on a conventional base would be quite misleading. For instance, if there was a precisely similar competing company that had bought its fixed asset in year 15, the earnings of such company would not be basically comparable because it would carry a depreciation charge 48 per cent greater.

It might seem quite simple to adjust for this factor; and indeed it would be under these highly simplified assumptions. However, in practice exactly the same distortion would apply but would be impossible to isolate and allow for, as any two corporations competing in practice have vast arrays of fixed assets purchased at various times.

Under current value accounting, these inter-company comparisons are basically valid; and the gross method has the particularly neat effect of showing the total increase in net worth of $142,200 divided logically into its two main constituent elements:

$ 88,200	as the accumulation of annual earnings
54,000	representing the profit attributable to the fact that the asset which was purchased for $100,000 now requires $154,000 to replace.
$142,200	

Moreover, this clear presentation occurs not only in the year the asset is completely written off, but throughout its useful life.

Inferences from this illustration

It is interesting to observe that this type of argument, which simply cannot be settled decisively in theory, is relatively easy to settle in practice. If the company had waited for the experts to solve this problem by discussion they would still be waiting. However, by proceeding, they succeeded in presenting an interesting new form of statement that most people would concede was more significant than the old type. Those who did not concur could easily reconstruct the old presentation.

There were few criticisms of the Imperial Tobacco statements, but there were those who insisted that this type of statement might not be satisfactory for all types of company. In point of fact, somewhat similar ideas have been worked out successfully in a variety of different types of companies. There may be some circumstances in which the plan would not yield satisfactory results; but anyone really interested in advancing the accounting art would make a much more solid contribution by finding out that this was actually the case in such circumstances, rather than by entrenching himself behind a dogmatic position under the inspiration of a sort of divine revelation.

If good results are not obtained in some attempted application, it is entirely likely that some better method will be evolved in the attempt.

Standardization or flexibility?

It might be useful to return to the question of standardization in the light of the foregoing discussion. It may be remembered that it was suggested in a previous chapter that one of the hottest arguments currently raging between accountants revolves round the question of the extent to which we should seek an authoritative uniformity as opposed to encouraging flexibility.

This is one of those drearily inconclusive questions with plenty of good arguments on both sides. There is no foreseeable conclusion to it. In fact, perhaps it does not matter too much. In a practical way, if it became popular for companies to provide their statements in what they considered the most informative manner, with supplementary data to reconcile to generally accepted principles, there might be much less steam in this flexibility-versus-uniformity debate. If a company were encouraged to show what it felt was the best picture, would it worry so much about the conventional presentation that could be worked out by those who wanted it? It might be much easier to agree to the rigidities of uniformity in these circumstances.

Surely no one could object to different procedures where different circumstances warranted them. No one could possibly insist on, say, the same rules in valuing an inventory of low-priced perishable goods (such as bread) and of high-priced imperishable goods (such as diamonds). On the other hand, it will equally be admitted by any reasonable observer that accounting principles sometimes sanction several procedures of almost equal validity when one would do us. It is hard to believe much would be lost by agreeing that everyone would use the same rule in such cases.

In some measure the two schools of thought—that stressing the advantages of individual judgment and that stressing the advantages of uniformity—could both be satisfied if the conventional form of presentation were narrowed down more rigidly, and companies were encouraged to publish more comprehensive and informative statements of their own design.

Main statement versus footnotes

If a new type of statement is produced, and supplementary information is provided whereby such statement can be converted to conventional form, it is evident that the reverse procedure would be equally possible. In other words, statements could be produced in conventional form, with supplementary data provided in footnotes, to throw additional light on the company's operation. To an investment analyst, it would presumably not matter very much which form of presentation was adopted. However, if progress is really to be hoped for, it becomes quite important for companies to adopt the first method; that is, to produce the new form of statement, leaving the reconciliation of the conventional form to the footnotes and supplementary information. There are two reasons why this should be so. In the first place, if the company really feels the new presentation provides a better financial picture, it is important that such preference is indicated by using this presentation in the main body of the statements. Only in this way can the preference of those who have prepared the statements be definitely established.

Moreover, financial statements tend to be summarized in statistical services and produced in printed form in newspapers, and it is desirable that the new and better form of presentation should be thus broadcast. When a set of financial statements is written up in the press, a few key figures are usually extracted, and the cautionary information and footnotes tend to be dropped. If the new form of statement is really an improvement on the conventional form, to attempt to provide the new information in footnotes is really a cowardly evasion.

The language of analogy

So much emphasis has been placed on the similarity between language and accounting that it might seem fair to ask why improvement in accounting has to be made such an issue; why not let better forms come gradually just as improvements emerge in language from the writings of our good authors. The answer is, of course, that developments are rushing in too fast in the business world and the natural evolutionary processes must be greatly speeded up. Nevertheless, the language analogy does provide some interesting parallels. Presumably, improvements in language have never been produced by a congress of philologists gathered together to find out better ways of saying something. On the contrary, new phrases, new words, and new methods of expression tend to get developed by people who are in the process of doing something practical, that is, trying to communicate ideas rather than setting out to reach agreement on some theoretical improvement. For example, currently the astronauts have popularized the phrase "a go situation." This may not be a very useful or admirable invention in language, although some parents will welcome it as an alternative to "okay." However it is a practical illustration of general acceptance of a new form of expression that arose from practice rather than through any group effort at enriching the language.

The prerequisite of success

By far the most important contribution to better financial reporting would be a vigorous campaign of exploration and experiment based on a genuine desire to communicate full and accurate information, and an appreciation of the essentially pragmatic nature of accounting.

8

Practical Applications

IT SHOULD BE CLEAR by now that the aim of this text is to clarify the nature of financial reporting and to suggest a point of view and techniques that will lead to the production of better statements. It is not primarily concerned with promoting or defending specific reforms. Even the current valuation of fixed assets, which has served so frequently as a useful illustration, is not insisted on as a final answer. It appears to the author a generally more useful approach than the conventional original cost basis; but this conviction is subsidiary to the essential idea that we will produce better statements only if we really want to provide clear information and venture boldly into new forms of presentation with a complete grasp of the real nature of financial communication.

It is tempting to let matters stand at this point, but perhaps a detailed review of some of the common forms of presentation might be illuminating. In this hope, some possible applications are discussed in this chapter—taking the risk that specific examples may divert attention from the general theme to particular remedies intended only to be suggestive.

Even in such a review where specific balance sheet items are considered, the discussion has to be widely generalized. Accounting texts deal usually with the statements of manufacturing companies, although a relatively small proportion of published financial statements are for such companies. There are, in fact, so many other types of companies that it is perhaps dangerous to think of manufacturing company statements as normal or to generalize too confidently on this one type of statement—particularly as many important types of companies (such as banks, mines, insurance companies, oil producers, acceptance houses, railways, air lines, stock brokers, and many others) have quite different problems from manufacturing companies and from each other. An asset like land has quite different implications to a manufacturing company and to a real estate investment company.

There was a discussion in Chapter 6 of the unsuitability of commercial style accounting in non-profit organizations, and a somewhat analogous danger exists in applying rules blindly to one type of commercial organization that were worked out for another kind of enterprise.

It should be remembered that the following suggestions are based primarily on the manufacturing type of statements. This is merely on the grounds that we must start somewhere.

General format

It is hard to see much wrong with the general format of published annual statements—a balance sheet showing assets, liabilities, and the resultant ownership equity, together with a statement explaining the change in such equity since the previous balance sheet. While we must venerate no sacred cows, this seems a pretty reasonable presentation until someone comes up with something more informative.

Form of the balance sheet

The conventional balance sheet is supposed to be drafted to present the basic equation between assets, liabilities, and equity. Either in the form of assets equals liabilities plus equity, or assets minus liabilities equals equity. Sometimes this basic picture is blurred through failure to classify an important item, such as a reserve or accrual left in the twilight zone between liabilities and equity. Even when all items are properly classified in three sections, it does not necessarily follow that this presents the picture most likely to be generally useful. There is at least one other reasonable alternative. Assets can be regarded as amounts entrusted to custody, and "liabilities" considered sources of capital. Thus trade payables are treated as an involuntary contribution of capital by the company's suppliers, and accumulated depreciation (as another source of capital earmarked out of prior year earnings) goes over to the right-hand side of the balance sheet. This pattern can be set up in conventional balance sheet form but is perhaps more easily handled as two separate statements: one for assets and the other for sources of capital.

A rather different sort of picture can be developed from this approach. Is it an improvement? We will find out only if it is generally considered so after someone tries it in practice.

Presentation of working capital position

It is accepted practice to show current assets and current liabilities, to give some indication of the liquidity of the enterprise—one of the items of greatest importance in balance sheet presentation. Except for net income, the working capital position is more often referred to in a company's annual report than any other item. However, conventional presentation produces an almost meaningless conglomeration. The assets included are a mixture of two quite different sorts of item. There is, on the one hand, cash resources, such as cash itself, marketable securities held as a temporary investment, or short-term loans. These assets are of quite a different nature to the genuinely working assets of receivables and inventories, and adding together the two types of item produces a total of almost no significance.

Consider a simple case. At successive year ends, suppose a company's working capital was as follows:

Start of year:		
Cash	$ 1,000,000	
Receivables	20,000,000	
Inventories	30,000,000	
Marketable securities	10,000,000	$ 61,000,000
Bank loans	2,000,000	
Payables	15,000,000	17,000,000
Working capital		$ 44,000,000
End of year:		
Cash	$ 1,000,000	
Receivables	40,000,000	
Inventories	60,000,000	
Marketable securities	2,000,000	$103,000,000
Bank loans	25,000,000	
Payables	30,000,000	55,000,000
		$ 48,000,000

On this basis the directors can report that working capital has increased by $4,000,000—and this sounds reassuring.

But can anyone pretend that this presents a fair picture of the company's relative liquidity?

A simple rearrangement could be made to show a much clearer picture. One way to do this would be to separate the cash and cash resources from the assets genuinely at work. For example:

Start of year:		
Cash	$ 1,000,000	
Marketable securities	10,000,000	
	11,000,000	
Bank loans	2,000,000	
Cash resources		$ 9,000,000
Receivables	20,000,000	
Inventories	30,000,000	
	50,000,000	
Less: Payables	15,000,000	
Net working assets		35,000,000
Working capital		$44,000,000
End of year:		
Cash	$ 1,000,000	
Marketable securities	2,000,000	
	3,000,000	
Bank loans	25,000,000	
Cash resources (deficit)		($22,000,000)
Receivables	40,000,000	
Inventories	60,000,000	
	100,000,000	
Payables	30,000,000	
Net working assets		70,000,000
Working capital		$48,000,000

These are the same figures, but the fact is emphasized that while working capital has gone up $4,000,000, this is the result of committing an additional $35,000,000 (net) to receivables and inventories and at the same time turning surplus cash resources of $9,000,000 to a debt position of $22,000,000. From the point of view of liquidity the company's position has thus deteriorated by $31,000,000.

It might be noted that no immediate conclusions can be safely jumped to on the basis of these figures. The significant fact is that during the year the receivables and inventories have doubled. The important question is: Has this resulted from increased business or from poor control over collections and purchasing? The revised presentation simply indicates more clearly the main change in liquid resources, and thus indicates the most important line of further inquiry.

Assets

In listing assets, two questions arise: form of presentation and valuation. "Valuation" has tended to acquire a technical sense in accounting, for reasons already explained, and this is perhaps the most unfortunate development in the history of accounting. Whatever the difficulties involved, we must attempt to move closer to economic facts, and our "values" must be brought as close to realistic current values as we can get them.

Comments on some of the more frequently encountered assets follow.

1. Cash. Normally this presents no valuation problem, as valuation problems arise only when we try to state non-cash assets at their cash equivalent. Nor are there serious problems of presentation. The current tendency to state all cash, bank, loan, and overdraft balances as one consolidated item is a good one. All that can be expected from a balance sheet is a very general picture, and it is simply distracting to show several deposit and loan balances—unless there is some special good reason to do so.

2. Marketable securities. It is common for companies to carry surplus funds temporarily in the form of marketable securities. The convention is that these securities should be carried at cost, with the current market value shown in parenthesis. If current market values drop materially below cost, it is usual to write the securities down to market.

It is easy to recognize in this conventional treatment the outworn conservatism of "the lower of cost or market." It would be much clearer if these securities were always carried at market—as long as there is a genuine market for the quantity held. In exceptional cases the quoted prices would not be the price at which a large holding of securities could actually be liquidated, and in such cases the quoted price might not provide the appropriate valuation. However, in the typical case, market values would be the significant information that any reader of a balance sheet would wish to have.

If a manufacturing company holds a large portfolio of marketable securities for a considerable period of time, to show securities on the balance sheet at cost, even with market values in parenthesis, could quite seriously distort the income position of the company. For many manufacturing companies, the holding of such securities is a normal feature of their operations, and consequently any profits or losses on disposal should be considered part of the normal earnings of the company. But this cannot be accomplished satisfactorily if securities are carried at cost, as was demonstrated by an actual example presented in Chapter 5.

Carrying such securities at market also gives a more accurate picture of liquid resources and working capital.

In view of all the advantages of adjusting such securities to market price, it may be wondered why the tendency has been to adhere to cost. It is simply an illustration of the unsatisfactory adherence to a rigid concept of profit realization: that profit is realized only when a sale is made. This probably is a pretty good rule, and indeed is as satisfactory as any, when dealing with the sale of merchandise in the ordinary course of trade. However, the automatic extension of this realization principle to the sale of securities, held as a temporary investment of cash, makes very little sense.

As far as presentation goes, a good argument could be made for combining marketable securities with cash in one total under some such heading as "Cash Resources." This is really the figure that a reader of the balance sheet would normally be interested in. Whether temporarily surplus funds are invested in securities, or left on deposit, or on call loan, or in some other readily available form, is a question of cash management. The segregation of marketable securities on the balance sheet would not appear to provide enlightenment on this aspect of the company's operations.

These observations do not necessarily apply to marketable securities held by companies whose business is investment or life insurance or any other activity in which the investment of funds is one of the main objects rather than a side-line. Each one of these special cases would require consideration in the light of its particular function.

3. Non-marketable securities. Securities that are not marketable are of course not properly shown as current assets.

The valuation of such securities often presents one of the most difficult problems in balance sheet preparation. There are so many different circumstances that it is impossible to generalize.

One usage already sanctioned, when dealing with subsidiary companies, is to carry the investment at cost adjusted to reflect changes in equity since acquisition. This is at least likely to be more helpful than unadjusted cost. There would seem little reason to object to the extension of this method to minority holdings. However, the treatment of these very difficult cases pretty well has to be left to judgment in each case according to its circumstances. The only solid conclusion is that the aim should be to present the best notion of current value that can be given.

4. Receivables. In the presentation of receivables, companies have sometimes been encouraged to give considerable break-downs to distinguish between receivables from customers, from affiliated companies, from officers and employees, and so on. There can be little general interest in such break-downs unless there is some special reason for them. They are probably overdone.

Also misguided was the common emphasis on the desirability of disclosing the amount of the provision for bad and doubtful debts. This is a significant figure only to someone who has made a serious study of the accounts. Moreover, setting up a provision for receivables is simply an alternative procedure to writing down the accounts, and the only figure of any genuine significance is the net amount of receivables less provision; any detail beyond this is simply part of the mechanics of establishing the net realizable value of the accounts.

When establishing a balance sheet value for receivables, it would seem logical to take into account not only questions of ultimate collectability, but also the time factor. Even the best receivables cannot be as valuable as cash on the balance sheet date, and this is a fact of importance. In preparing a balance sheet, we add all sorts of different types of asset together, and the only theory on which such a procedure can be supported is that all assets are converted to a similar basis of value—or as nearly a similar basis as can be managed. The common denominator is, of course, cash equivalent. Receivables, like all other non-cash assets, should be stated as nearly as possible to the value that the company would be willing to accept for them in cash at the balance sheet date.

5. Prepaid expenses. It is a pity prepaid expenses are normally such a small item on most balance sheets as they are perhaps the item on which accountants have lavished most care and ingenuity. About the only thing that need be said of them is that the usual procedures for establishing the unexpired portion of such items as taxes and insurance afford a good example of the sort of techniques that can be developed when we set our heart to the task.

6. Inventories. There are a great many cases in which inventory valuation is one of the most important points in the entire financial statement—both in its effect on earnings and on liquid position. Yet inventory valuation is at present in a state of confusion even in theory. Apart from theoretical difficulties, there are many areas of doubt in the procedures by which inventories are actually priced in practice.

The main problems in inventory valuation are the problems of coping with changes in price level and of recognizing obsolescence. When prices remain stable and there is no question of obsolescence, cost provides a reasonably clear, well-understood, and satisfactory basis for inventory valuation. However, if there are price changes, or if obsolescence is a factor, important issues are raised that have not yet been satisfactorily settled.

In very simple situations, price changes can be handled quite easily. As demonstrated in an example in Chapter 5, when a price change occurs the inventory should be carried at the new price; this is now the rule for downward revisions and, in all logic, should be the rule when prices rise. However, many actual cases are not simple. The balance sheet date will find goods in various stages of manufacture and located at different points in the distribution system. All sorts of complicating factors must be coped with. What is of paramount importance is some general overriding objective, and this is perhaps provided by the accounting concept of "matching" costs against revenue.

This concept may not have had the careful discussion and definition it requires. At times it has been used as an excuse by accounting apologists who feel that the balance sheet we produce requires some explanation. The suggestion is that the balance sheet is not a valuation document, nor intended to be one, but simply a collection of residual balances left over after an immensely valuable process of "matching costs and revenues" to produce the income statement.

Dubious as the foregoing argument is, there is merit in the matching concept. It is based on the clear precept that periodic profit can best be measured by taking the revenue for the period and deducting from it the expenses laid out to earn such revenue. In practice this is often not as simple as it sounds but it does provide a good basic objective.

Inventories are a device whereby we attempt to slice up the profit earned by an enterprise so that appropriate amounts are attributed to each period. The final valuation of an inventory must therefore be reached by writing off the cost of what has contributed to or been caused by the operations of the current period and carrying forward the amounts that are expected to contribute to the following period.

The essential idea is that each financial period should stand on its own feet. Thus write-offs that result from errors in the past (such as overpurchasing) should be charged against the earlier period and not carried forward. The objective should be that management starts out the new period with a chance to earn a normal profit in that period—unencumbered by errors of the past and without benefit of brilliant past achievements. There is no other principle in inventory valuation of comparable importance, and it is essential that this concept should be given full weight. Through an old rule of so-called conservatism, the basic notion in inventory valuation is supposed to be the valuing of inventory at the lower of cost or market. As suggested in a previous chapter, this sort of conservative rule might well have served usefully when the balance sheet was the only important statement, and an appraisal of credit the only important objective. However, if we accept as a basic rule that a realistic and useful profit figure for each period must be produced, the lower of cost or market ceases to make any sense.

A great deal of work has been done by way of research to refine the lower-of-cost-or-market concept, but no satisfactory official code of rules has been generally accepted; and it may well be that the basic confusion of the old rule about anticipating losses but not profits is the reason the issue remains confused.

When you get down to details in inventory valuation, a great many practical decisions arise regarding what costs should be inventoried and what costs should be written off. For example, what about the cost of freight from the factory to a sales warehouse? This sort of item should be judged by deciding which period is likely to be benefitted. If the probability is that the goods will actually be needed at the warehouse to which they have been shipped, it would seem clear that the cost of such freight should be inventoried and thus carried forward to the new period. On the other hand, if an error of judgment has been made and goods have been shipped to a warehouse in excess of what is expected to be needed there, there is justification for charging off the cost to the earlier period when the error of judgment was made. This simple illustration may serve to indicate one of the many instances where judgment must come into the preparation of good financial statements. Here is clearly a matter of opinion.

The whole problem of obsolescence bristles with judgmental situations. The extent to which goods are obsolete is one on which very wide opinions may be held. Here again it is better to encourage the use of judgment than to try to impose illogical rules. The significant point is that, if a problem arises on which there is doubt about valuation and on which different opinions may reasonably be formed, it makes it impossible for satisfactory statements to be produced if the accountant attempts to hide behind some kind of cut-and-dried rule of thumb because if there is genuine doubt, no rule of thumb can possibly be expected to give reliable results.

Direct costing is an attractive method of inventory valuation for tax purposes, as it defers tax payments as long as possible. It also has some appeal for those who still consider that conservatism has merit; that is, to those who feel that, in cases of doubt, it is always safer to write off an expenditure than to carry it forward.

The idea in direct costing is to write off all overhead cost against operations and carry forward only cost of material and direct labour. It can be said in praise of this theory that it was a good corrective to the previous practice that encouraged the spreading of all overheads blindly and automatically over the goods produced, regardless of whether such goods were sold during the period or carried forward in the inventory. In short, we face here the question of whether, and to what extent, overhead costs should be carried forward. It is pretty difficult to escape the conclusion that overhead is part of the cost (and therefore of the value) of goods. The only question is, how much overhead should be carried forward. It would be wrong, of course, to carry forward excessive overhead caused by bad management, errors of judgment, or even acts of God in the previous period. However, through proper standard costing, in anything but very unusual circumstances, it should be possible to make an estimate of the amount of overhead that should be properly carried forward, so that the new period can start off on the right foot.

7. Fixed asset valuation. The valuation of fixed assets has been discussed at various points throughout this text and the prejudices of the author have been pretty well exposed. They will not be reiterated here.

8. Goodwill. No even vaguely adequate solution has been found for the accounting presentation of goodwill. This is a genuine and easily recognized asset, but it has proved so difficult to get a satisfactory basis for valuing it that accountants have tended to encourage writing it off as fast as possible. Undoubtedly the incorporeal nature of goodwill is part of the trouble, suggesting as it does some sort of lack of respectability as an asset. Although it may be wondered if the patient amortization of an old building long past its real usefulness should be any less painful to the accounting conscience.

In any event, current treatment of goodwill is about as unsatisfactory as it could possibly be. It is normally only recorded if purchased—which does not make sense—and it is written off or carried forward quite arbitrarily.

If no attempt is made to value this asset, there is something to be said for writing it off completely.

One approach to the subject is to work out the net book value of all assets and liabilities other than goodwill and then compare the result with the market value of the company's shares. This gives, in effect, the value placed on the company's goodwill by the market. The extent to which this sort of calculation is valid is determined, of course, by the accuracy with which the other assets are valued. One obvious drawback of the method is that, in a sense, it begs the question entirely. The accountant uses the investor's valuation of the enterprise to prepare his statements—instead of giving the investor a statement that will help him to make his valuation. However, this approach at least brings out clearly what the investor is paying for goodwill if he buys stock on the market—a most interesting consideration.

Liabilities

The standard practice of dividing liabilities between long and short term is clearly sound. On the other hand, the further break-down of current liabilities into various classifications seems pointless. Overdrafts and demand loans should be netted with cash resources, and all other items could be included in one total unless there is some special circumstance that requires disclosure. The distinction between accrued liabilities and accounts payable is a technical one of no significance to most balance sheet readers. To segregate taxes from other payables does indicate the extent of privileged claims, but this is normally of interest only when there is a danger of imminent bankruptcy.

For the general view that can be expected from a balance sheet, a neater and clearer picture is presented if the statement is not cluttered up with irrelevant details.

The real problem in regard to liabilities lies in deciding what liabilities should be recognized. There used to be some disposition to consider that only strictly legal liabilities should be provided for, but this is too restrictive a view. The growing tendency is to recognize de facto liabilities as well. In practice it is hard to know where to draw the line. A difficult case is presented, for example, by the fact that many companies have a policy of paying pensions to employees even where no formal pension plan exists, or to supplement pensions under a formal plan that are not deemed to be adequate. Normally it is not considered necessary to set up a liability for these ex gratia pensions, on the grounds that they may be stopped at any time at the company's option. While this is true, in practice the stopping of such payments would be a very serious step, and indeed the consequences might be so damaging to staff morale that it would be almost out of the question. It could be argued that such payments are in effect practical obligations and should therefore be part of the financial position.

Long-term contracts and leases have sometimes raised questions. It is not uncommon for leases to cover long periods and thus to require heavy payments in future. If the company went out of business or became unprofitable, these payments might become a factor of crucial importance. However companies have a great many such continuing contracts and it would become hopelessly confusing if all of them were disclosed. The basic assumption in published statements is that the company is a going concern. Hence, unless there is some special reason for calling attention to a particular contract, it should not be necessary to do so. The special circumstances calling for disclosure would normally arise from departures from ordinary commercial practices.

A specially interesting problem is presented by the newer types of lease-back agreements where the lessee obtains the right to purchase the property at the end of the lease for a nominal sum. While technically this is simply a lease with an option to purchase, it is more in the nature of a purchase with extended terms for payment, because the stated purchase price is not really the consideration for which ownership will change hands. The real purchase consideration is included in what are technically the rental payments.

There are two ways of accounting for lease-backs. The legal terms can be followed by treating the rental payments in the normal way, or the value of the building may be set up as an asset—as though the property had actually been purchased—and the liability for rentals set up as though these constituted a mortgage repayable in annual instalments. There is here a choice between following legal and economic concepts, and the tendency is more and more to prefer the latter. This can be justified on the grounds that financial statements are intended to be used to assess performance and strength, and these are questions of economics rather than of legal relationships. If the asset-liability approach is adopted in such cases, the legal position should, of course, be disclosed too, presumably in a footnote.

Income statement

Published income statements have not settled into such a standardized pattern as balance sheets. Two figures of basic importance should be disclosed: total revenue and net profit. These are in effect the indicators of volume and profitability without which an appreciation of a company's performance could not be attempted.

There are several different approaches to determining how the intermediary figures for expenditures and other items should be grouped between total revenue and net profit, so as to set forth the most informative presentation. It is possible only to suggest some of the considerations that should be weighed.

1. Revenue. While total revenue must be disclosed, in many cases it is not in itself adequate. Where a company handles a wide variety of products (and this is increasingly the case), the revenue figure should be broken down by product line to give a complete picture.

2. Expenses. Expenses may be classified in various ways. The original idea of first deducting manufacturing costs to produce what was called "gross" profit has become less popular. Certainly the notion that manufacturing costs are more basic or essential than selling or administrative expense is hard to justify in logic. It can also be questioned whether it is sensible to give income taxes the very special prominence they usually are accorded. These taxes are based on profits before tax, but this does not necessarily imply that they are any less genuinely operating expenses than other necessary expenditures. It is difficult however to generalize much further in this area.

The foregoing discussion of specific items is intended to illustrate the confusion that has crept into accounting conventions through lack of clear-headedness. This is, of course, not intended as an exhaustive discussion of any of these items, but only as indicative of the sort of improvements that could be worked out if companies were encouraged to experiment.

9

The Essential Element of Human Judgment

MOST ACCOUNTANTS entered or were pushed into their professional careers because they were good at mathematics. This reflects the unshakable conviction of those outside the profession that accounting is essentially a matter of formulas, rules, and calculations of petty exactitude and grinding routine. When accountants point out that the preparation of statements is an exciting and absorbingly interesting pursuit, full of opportunities for imagination and creative flair, this is simply taken as conclusive proof of how dessicated and removed from normal warm-hearted human interests they actually are.

Accountants themselves soon learn that there are no mathematics involved in accounting beyond addition and subtraction, but there is nothing wrong (status-wise) with mathematics, and they come to connive at the fiction that this form of intellectual effectiveness is at the basis of their profession. It is nevertheless true, as accountants keep insisting, that the preparation of statements is quite as much a judgmental process as a statistical one.

Where judgment comes in

It is probably impossible for anyone who has not gone through the process of preparing a complicated set of statements to appreciate how much judgment is required, and to what a limited extent it is a question of following laid-down or logically derived rules. However, one illustration from inventory valuation will be ventured in an attempt to make the point.

As a background for this case, it should be remembered that to produce a reasonably meaningful financial statement always involves difficulties of inventory valuation. Not only is there commonly a very large number of items, but these vary enormously in nature—the durable and the perishable, the cheap and the expensive, goods subject to styling and goods not, and so on—and a great many different approaches to valuation are called for by the varying nature of the goods.

In an attempt to simulate the valuation process let us consider just one case: an appliance manufactured at a cost of \$80 and listed to sell at \$100. Let us assume this appliance is of a sort for which new annual models appear each year on July 1. In such cases, sales demand naturally tends to be high when new models come out; and if, in the interest of economical operations, the company wishes to maintain sales volume steadily throughout the year, it is necessary to reduce prices gradually by mark-downs, special sales, discounts, or other devices—no one could be expected to pay full list prices in the month of June with new models just about to come out. To oversimplify the case, suppose it is estimated that sales may be reasonably sustained throughout the year by dropping the list price by $10 each quarter, so that the appliance sells at $100 during the first quarter, $90 during the second, $80 during the third, and $70 during the fourth.

The normal rule is to value inventory at cost, which is $80 in this case. However, this would mean that the statements would show $20 per unit profit during the first quarter, $10 per unit during the second, a break-even in the third, and $10 per unit loss in the fourth. But this makes absolutely no sense if each quarter shows equally good sales performance.

One reasonable solution to this case is to estimate the average selling price during the year and to take into profit each quarter the average profit per unit for the year on the number of units sold during the quarter. This seems sensible, but it involves estimating sales, and if sales run over or under the estimate a quite complicated adjustment can be required. If a practical case of this kind is tackled, it will be found that there are often no established rules for guidance and that an almost endless variety of different factors can enter in.

It is easy for anyone to picture the great variety of goods in a department store and to imagine the problems of inventory-taking there. While this may represent an extreme example of complexity, all large corporations have a great variety of valuation problems.

The net effect of such complexity and variety is that detailed formulas and rules simply cannot be laid down to cover all contingencies. Intelligence and ingenuity must be continually exercised; this in turn means that there is always lots of room for differences of opinion on procedures and valuations.

Accounting textbooks tend to concentrate entirely on principles, rules, and regulations—in short, on what might be called the mechanics of statement preparation—and to ignore the human considerations that enter into the process from the simple fact that statements are designed and prepared by human beings for interpretation and use by other human beings.

A complete and balanced view of the problems involved in financial reporting cannot possibly be gained if the very important human elements are ignored. It is therefore necessary to attempt a brief dissertation on some implications of this neglected factor.

Management preoccupations

To begin with, as financial statements are essentially reports by management to shareholders and other outsiders, we might consider the statements firstly from the point of view of management.

Management's first concern is to manage successfully. In our competitive society this is seldom an easy task. Clearly it is even more difficult if management is interfered with or forced to work with a feeling of someone constantly watching every move waiting for an opportunity to criticize. No one can work well in these circumstances. The way to keep shareholders happy and minimize interference from them is to operate profitably, and if possible to keep reporting higher profits each year. In pursuit of this goal, each year's profit becomes a mark that must be exceeded the following year. All this adds up to the fact that the most desirable pattern for management to aim at is one of reporting gradually increasing profits.

Suppose a company has the following earnings experience:

Year	*Profit*
1	$500,000
2	900,000
3	300,000
4	700,000

The average profits during this period are $600,000. Consider the problem of preparing statements at the end of year 2 and at the end of year 3. On the former occasion a very substantial increase in profits has been earned and on the latter occasion a drastic decrease in profits. It is simply human nature to set about establishing values in each of these circumstances in a somewhat different frame of mind. In the highly profitable year, one can expect an anxiety not to overdo it by reporting profits too high; while at the end of a poor year, it would be natural to look for anxiety in the other direction, that is, a tendency not to want to make things look "any worse than they are."

This instinctive bias of even the most honest reporters presents one of the hardest problems to cope with in financial reporting—in some ways more difficult to handle than deliberate fraud or false principles.

It is no service to the cause of progress in reporting to gloss over this basic problem.

Codification of principles or rules

In the light of these observations it might be well to reconsider the possibility of writing an authoritative statement of accounting principles that would provide guidance in the difficult situations mentioned above.

In view of the difficulties, it is natural enough that we should seek certainty and clarification, but as suggested several times in the course of this text, it is very doubtful if a code would provide the answer we seek.

To begin with, from the way some accountants talk, one would think that no statement of accepted principles now exists. Yet every accounting text is in effect an attempt to codify accounting principles. True enough, the principles are those believed to be valid by the authors, not the concerted opinion of the whole accounting profession—much less that of the entire financial community, all the members of which have some interest in the subject. However, a code must be written by someone, and many of the good texts are team efforts. For example, *Montgomery's Auditing,*[1] an outstanding text over the years, is published in successive editions by the partners of his firm and, one would imagine, probably by as competent a group effort as our accounting institutes would likely be able to organize. Incidentally, in this text a chapter is devoted to each item in the financial statements and each chapter has a section specifically stating the accounting principles that apply to that item—resulting in over 150 pages being devoted specifically to stating what accepted accounting principles are.

Even these voluminous texts do not provide specific rules that would guide the accountant in the vast majority of the varied situations he encounters in the course of preparing a set of statements.

The problems of theoretical agreement

Apart from the general difficulty of providing sufficiently detailed rules, there is the basic problem of securing general

[1] Norman J. Lenhart, C.P.A., and Philip L. Defliese, C.P.A. (8th ed.; New York: The Ronald Press Co., 1957).

agreement to theoretical statements. After all, those drafting the rules are human beings too. Even when a group is pretty well in agreement, the actual drafting of a group pronouncement is never easy.

This fact has been demonstrated again and again in the past. Perhaps the most brilliant and distinguished group ever collected together was a study group under the auspices of the Rockefeller Foundation and the AICPA. The group had forty-four members and tackled the subject of income. Their report [2] under the distinguished editorship of George O. May was the result of four years of discussion and study. The 160 pages of the report make fascinating reading but it is interesting to notice that its conclusions, which ran to 7 pages, were followed by 30 pages of additional observations by individual members—8 pages labelled "Dissent" and 8 labelled "Comments" (the latter title implying at least the conviction that further explanation was called for).

It would seem safe to conclude two things. In the first place, any statement that could be drawn up would be unlikely to be very different from what we already have and, in the second place, it is not conceivable that this sort of thing can materially narrow down the wide area where judgment (and therefore diversity) must hold sway.

In summary, while it is understandable that accountants should yearn for an authoritative code to help them in their difficulties, the wish is somewhat escapist in character, born of a desire to hide from the realities.

Accounting Courts

An interesting suggestion was contributed to this discussion by Leonard Spacek in an article in *The Accounting*

[2] *Concepts of Business Income* (New York: The Macmillan Co., Publishers, 1952).

Review that advocated the establishment of an Accounting Court. The gist of the idea may be inferred from these extracts:

> From a professional point of view, we need the case method of arriving at decisions on accounting principles.
>
> The accounting court, as I visualize it would adopt the "utilitarian concept" of authority for accounting principles based on economic facts specifically explained.
>
> I would assume that such rules would be similar to those followed in the United States Supreme Court or any other body where decisions are logically based on briefs and arguments.
>
> Government regulatory bodies would argue their views before the accounting court. But this court would be a professional court, not a court of law; hence its decisions would not affect the laws nor the administration of the laws by regulatory bodies.
>
> The knowledge of accounting techniques would be of secondary importance in the qualifications of such judges.[3]

The plan envisages sponsorship by the AICPA and preliminary hearings before the Committee on Accounting Procedure of that institute.

It is good to have a few bright ideas in this dark and difficult area, but it is hard to escape the conclusion that the Judges in such a Court would be under the same difficulties as a committee setting out to draft a statement of accounting principles.

When one considers the ponderous nature of court procedure, it is difficult to imagine much progress through this device, although it is easy to predict some fascinating arguments.

[3] Leonard Spacek, C.P.A., "The Need for an Accounting Court," *The Accounting Review* (American Accounting Association), July, 1958.

The reader's point of view

As mentioned above, the fact also seems to get overlooked that financial statements are read by human beings. This suggests a further area for investigation—the manner in which, say, an investor goes about reading a statement and what he expects to get from it.

It is surprising how little the decision-making processes of the investor appear to have been studied by accountants. It is often insisted that a balance sheet and income statement must appear in every prospectus for the protection of the investor; in other words, so he can come to an informed opinion on whether the stock offered is a good buy. Yet it is difficult to imagine how the statements will lead him towards a reliable conclusion if they do not even attempt to place a valuation on the concern.

In studying the investment decision process, let us again dismiss from our minds the problems of the uninformed layman. He needs help, but it is no service to him to get him trying to value his investments by his own research. If he is uninformed, he should seek the advice of someone who is informed. Our problem is confined to providing information that will be intelligible to a serious analyst.

The analyst's job is to come to some reasonable conclusion as to what securities should be bought or sold at a given moment. It is often somewhat glibly said that financial statements aid him in coming to his conclusions; but to what extent do they aid him? A still more difficult question is: To what extent could they be made to aid him? In other words, what are the limitations?

However skilful or experienced an investment analyst is, his ultimate conclusions must inevitably be guess-work to some extent. Even if every shred of information about a company was made available and was fed into a computer and presented in fully digested form, a large element of luck would still remain in the decision. What the investment analyst is trying to decide is whether a certain security is likely to be worth more or less in the future than it is now. There are many predictable elements in the calculation; but the weather, the death of a key executive, the reconciliation of a misunderstanding with an important customer, and many more, completely unforeseeable, factors may influence a company's future development—and therefore may affect the value of its shares.

The problem for the investment analyst is to consider as many of the facts as can be made available, and to estimate the probable degree of success a company will have from this information. If he does his work properly, he will narrow down the area of guess-work, and his opinion will be correspondingly more valuable than that of someone who has no information at all to go on. This does not necessarily mean that he will always be right and the uninformed plunger always wrong; the probability, however, is that the analyst will be right oftener because of his studies.

Financial statements come into the picture because it is assumed that past performance is some indication of what future performance may be. Take the balance sheet for example. If a company has a strong asset position, it is more likely to be a successful company in future than if it has a precarious asset position, because solvency is an important quality in a company.

The trend of past earnings also provides some basis for estimating what is likely to happen in the future. A company with steadily growing sales and profits is probably a better bet for future expansion than a company whose sales and profits have been declining. All that the accountant can do for the investment analyst is to see that the financial facts of the company—its present position and the past trends—are presented as honestly and clearly as possible. No matter how much the statements are improved, there will never be any automatic way in which future developments can be predicted by studying statements alone; but the better the statements are, the more it will be possible to make reasonable estimates of future probabilities.

The conventional annual financial statements are, of course, not the only factual information available to the analyst. The pattern of shareholdings and many other significant areas can be presented factually and studied. Appraisals of the ability of key executives can be made at least partly with scientific techniques, and a wealth of other material may be collected, sorted out, and studied. All of this does not end up placing the analyst in a position to make a completely scientific prediction, but it does narrow down the area of guessing.

What the analyst wants from the accountant is not something guaranteed or incontrovertible. There can be no communicating worth bothering about except by a process of estimating and selecting assumptions. However, the analyst is surely entitled to expect that the assumptions will be selected with a view to making the resulting conclusions as useful as possible for his purpose.

This is a glaringly inadequate discussion of the human factor, but it does perhaps point to an area that requires much more thought and analysis. It is simply not good enough to say that financial statements help people to value their investments and leave it at that. We must look into the valuation process much more closely so that we can be sure we understand what sort of information would be most helpful.

In defence of subjective judgments

It has been argued in a previous chapter that objectivity is largely unattainable in financial reporting. No one could draw much useful information from the meagre sort of statements that could be prepared by anyone who confined himself to using only actual cash transactions. Judgment has to enter in; and while this inescapably opens the door for fraudulent manipulation or just plain poor judgment, it is not for that reason necessarily desirable to confine the use of judgment. It has already been shown that in fixed asset valuation, even if cost is adhered to, the rate of amortization must nevertheless be almost completely arbitrary —and thus depreciated value has a large discretionary element anyway. In these circumstances, it must be better to accept the essentially judgmental character of financial statements and, instead of trying to pin judgment down to the minimum area possible, to accept the fact that judgment is necessary and to concentrate on assuring that good and honest judgment is used.

There are many ways in which we could promote better judgment and assure ourselves of better statements, but there is not any magic formula that will abolish all our difficulties.

It would of course be helpful if we kept before us the basic purpose we are after: the preparation of useful information about values. Once this becomes a clear goal, uncluttered by some of our cherished myths, valuable guidance would be given to those coping with problems. It would also promote better statements if we dealt more effectively with those convicted of improper practices.

It should be noted that any encouragement of the use of more judgment and opinion (and correspondingly less reliance on established rules) would greatly complicate the task of the public accountant required to report whether, in his opinion, a statement presents fairly the financial position of a company. However, by the same token, such a trend would greatly enhance the role of the public accountant and his usefulness.

10

Concepts of Value and Income

IT WOULD BE hard to put the fundamental problem in financial reporting more clearly than it was put by Dr. Paton in the opening paragraphs of one of his splendid texts:

> In a broad sense accounting has one primary function: facilitating the *administration of economic activity. This function has two* closely related phases: (1) *measuring* and arraying economic data; (2) *communicating* the results of this process to interested parties. It follows that the job of accounting is being well done when those concerned are being supplied with significant, essential data, presented and interpreted in such manner as to promote understanding and a realistic, constructive pattern of decisions.
>
> This conception of accounting needs emphasis, particularly in view of the developments of recent years. Accounting, like other fields, is plagued with fetishes and sacred cows, and it is high time that homage be shifted from these to the underlying objective. Where recognition of economic reality runs counter to some convention or tradition, perhaps never soundly grounded, tradition should give way. . . . What is needed is a clear perception of the

basic function, and a willingness to review conventional ideas, terms and techniques in the light of such function.[1]

These are words that must be heeded. They come from one of the most respected authorities in accounting history.

Perhaps the first questions to consider are: How far do we fall short of this good advice? How far do we allow ourselves to become absorbed in paying homage to our sacred cows—to the neglect of our primary function of "facilitating the administration of economic activity"?

Here is one opinion:

> It has to be admitted that accountants are not agreed on the way in which income is to be defined. It follows, therefore, that even if there were no deliberate manipulation, an outsider (including most shareholders) cannot know the principles on which the figure is calculated. What information is he given? First, a profit-and-loss account that need not be complete, and tells us little about cash receipts and payments. This is supported by a statement called a balance sheet, which those writers who are wisest call "a list of ledger balances", but which nine members of the public out of ten think is a statement of assets, liabilities, and capital bearing some relationship to the worth of the business. The figure of income, given without explanations, is dependent on the figures in the balance sheet, some of which are related in a definite way to current prices, others less definitely; a third group are mere statements of money paid; and, worst of all, some of the figures may represent payments less deductions whose amounts are not disclosed.[2]

Then again, accountants themselves have been critical of their own efforts. A writer in an English professional journal points out:

[1]William A. Paton, Ph.D., C.P.A., *Essentials of Accounting* (New York: The Macmillan Co., Publishers, 1949), p. 1.

[2] Ronald S. Edwards, "The Nature and Measurement of Income," in W. J. Baxter and Sidney Davidson (eds.), *Studies in Accounting Theory* (London: Sweet & Maxwell, Ltd., Law Publishers, 1962). (Originally one of a series of articles appearing in *The Accountant,* July–October, 1938.)

> The most important of the many functions of the accountant, whether he be in public practice or in whole-time employment in industry, is perhaps the effective communication of his ideas and opinions to those whom they concern. Yet this all important aspect of the acountant's work is the one in which the profession has allowed itself most to be tied down by tradition and history and to which the leaders of the profession have devoted least effective attention.[3]

It should not surprise us that there is dissatisfaction because, if we examine orthodox accounting pronouncements, we must conclude that accountants have allowed themselves at times to be diverted from their essential task of being helpful to those interested in obtaining financial information, and have found themselves embarked on a variety of intellectually exhilarating but quite unprofitable wild goose chases. The profession has, of course, been earnestly trying to produce good statements. The trouble is that somewhere along the way we have got off the track, and we have come to think of good statements as statements conscientiously prepared according to rules we have (more or less) agreed on amongst ourselves. However admirable our intentions, this is not really very helpful and is certainly not our basic function.

This is such a crucial point that we must try to find how we could have got off the track so completely.

Our troubles started when we tried to come to grips with the elusive concept of value—so completely basic—along with what should be the closely related concept of profit. Here we started out with a somewhat simple sort of problem that gradually became more complicated as our economy developed. It is perhaps particularly difficult to detect the full implications of increasing complexity in a field like financial reporting in which one is apt to be absorbed in

[3] D. S. Anderson in *The Accountant,* October 13, 1962.

day-to-day problems and to be mainly concerned with finding handy solutions to new questions as they emerge, and thus to be less aware of long-term effects.

The accounting view of value

Whatever the variety of the needs of the different groups who read financial statements, we have seen that they must have one thing in common: they must want to know the value of the concern. This bedrock assumption was accepted naturally enough by early accountants. Absorbed as they were in problems of credit, they set before themselves the objective of producing a statement that would reliably establish the amount that could safely be lent to the concern—or to put it another way, to establish its financial strength. Owing, as we have seen previously, to the adoption of the policy of "conservatism" these early accountants found no insuperable difficulty in asset valuation. They produced statements that they could confidently feel understated values—and this was all that was required of them.

The accountant's worries about valuation began to develop as greater sophistication entered the picture with the growing interest in income determination, the added pressures introduced by income taxes, the growth of absentee ownership of corporations, the increasing complexity of business, the great increase in public investment in securities—in fact, with almost every development that took place.

All these trends combined to increase the importance of financial statements, and accountants found they had to take a more serious look at valuation problems. Rough-and-ready conservatively slanted valuations could be accepted for credit purposes, but the more demanding requirements of investors and tax collectors began to drive home some of the difficulties of valuation. As accountants strove with these difficulties, they began to understand what a tremendously complicated job asset valuation could be. For one thing they began to appreciate the essentially tentative nature of any system of valuation. When faced with the necessity of adding together apples and oranges, a common denominator must be developed on a basis of assumptions of some sort. With ingenuity, various solutions can usually be found, thus introducing the bothersome problem of diversity. There are usually several different ways of reaching an asset valuation, and quite often the choice between them can only be arbitrary.

In any event, the more they studied these problems the more accountants appreciated the tentative nature of the best of statements and, in the interests of honesty, their reservations were passed on to their clients. When accountants reported on statements, as we have already said, "the correct view" became "a correct view" and then "a fair view."

The result of growing doubts was an appreciation that the old self-confident affirmations somewhat oversimplified the situation. There were presumably only two courses open to a profession that considered honesty its corner-stone. Either a much more sophisticated and searching approach to valuation must be attempted or, alternatively, accountants must be careful to make clear to everyone the limitations of their relatively simple-minded approach to these problems. The former course would have been the most satisfactory solution ultimately, but the latter was much the easier way out and, moreover, it must at first have seemed to provide an adequate answer.

Of course, issues such as this do not come up in real life as dramatic choices to be made deliberately and decisively on the basis of all the facts involved. On the contrary, changes of this nature set in gradually—the twig being bent by a succession of little unrelated pressures developed by a vast number of small practical decisions. The important development was that accountants gradually came to accept the limitations of their products and to content themselves with making it clear what these limitations were.

The unfortunate part of taking the easy way out is that it is habit-forming. Ultimately accountants came to draw further and further away from the arena where the battle of our economic lives was being fought—further into a special world of their own, in which they made up their own rules.

This view may be found in any of the modern treatises or pronouncements. At first it was suggested that accountants should be careful to talk only of "book value" instead of value. Later even the term "book value" was frowned on as implying some sort of valuation process and we find the Terminology Committee of the AICPA warning accountants that "the term 'Ledger Balance' or a term such as 'The amount shown in published financial statements' would more clearly and accurately convey an exact meaning." This states correctly the current view. By then the profession had got around to subscribing to the doctrine that the balance sheet is not a valuation document at all. As put by *Terminology for Accountants* (a publication of The Canadian Institute of Chartered Accountants): "A balance sheet is a statement of current resources, unexpired costs, liabilities to be met and sources of ownership funds, rather than a statement of worth." This is now irreproachably orthodox dogma and could be supported by reference to other official pronouncements from the United States, England, or Canada.

Concepts of income

The question of valuation is basic not only to the balance sheet but to the perhaps even more important concept of "profit," as balance sheet values enter the determination of profit through the income account.

"Income" can be conceived of in several different ways. It would be possible, for example, to distinguish between the concepts of the accountant, the tax collector, the corporation lawyer, the economist, and the investment analyst. Which of these views should form the basis for financial reporting?

Fortunately it is fairly easy to eliminate the tax collector's and the lawyer's views for the purpose of this study. In Chapter 6, the relation between reported income and taxable income was considered, and the conclusion reached that taxable income can be left to follow reported income as based on generally accepted accounting principles. Much the same can be said for legal requirements. There are problems here, but not ones that affect our general line of reasoning.

Of the remaining concepts, the economist and the investment analyst have an essentially similar point of view. They want to know what the current value of a corporation is and whether it is increasing or decreasing. The big problem is to reconcile this concept with that of the accountant.

It is not surprising, as we have seen earlier, that the views of producer and user should be at variance; what is important is that they should be reconciled. The subject must not be dismissed by simply accepting the fact that the two sides have different points of view. If we are to get better statements, we must reach the best compromise possible between what the user would like and what the accountant can reasonably produce. In working out such a compromise, it is quite proper for the accountant to maintain that some of the requirements of the user are impossible to meet; what is certainly improper is that he should say that he does not intend even to attempt to meet the user's needs. More concretely, the accountant can qualify his valuations in any way he considers appropriate, but he cannot say he is not concerned with economic values or attempting to reach them.

Valuation—an essential approach

The problems of valuation, no matter how puzzling and baffling, must be tackled. They cannot be side-stepped.

One attempted evasion was to claim that investors were really not interested in balance sheet values so much as in net income. It was suggested that, although assets were carried in the balance sheet at amounts that did not represent their fair current value, this did not matter because the important statement was really not the balance sheet at all but the income statement. It was claimed that a satisfactory income statement could be constructed on the principle of "matching costs against revenues."

This will, of course, not do at all. The income statement includes the amortization or write-off of balance sheet values —quite often as a major item. If the balance sheet values are not defensible, the resulting net income is not defensible either. The "matching" of costs against revenues can be a useful device, but if it does not lead to a result that measures increase in value, it cannot claim to have any appropriateness.

The balance sheet and the income statement are best regarded not as two statements but as two parts of the same statement. They are inevitably tied together. The only sensible basis for a balance sheet is to attempt to show the worth of a company at a given date. By the same token, sensible basis for a balance sheet is to attempt to show the the extent to which the worth or value of a company has improved between balance sheet dates.

In short, the only acceptable basis for net income determination is the "better off" view. It is not useful to anyone to claim that a company has earned a net profit of $1,000,000 unless it can be demonstrated that its value has increased by that amount.

Measurable and unmeasurable factors

To insist on the necessity of measuring values in accounting—as best we can—is not to gloss over the difficulties that must be encountered in doing so. Asset measurement, in fact, requires every bit of ingenuity we can apply to it.

There is patently here no royal road to success. It will be found that different approaches will have to be adopted in valuing different kinds of assets if the best results are to be reached. There is no objection to the use of different approaches that are dictated by differences in the problem of valuing different kinds of assets; but for each type of asset the same approach must be applied consistently. Moreover, the same general objective must be in mind in the valuation of all types of assets: the objective of stating all assets at the best estimate of current values.

This latter principle is offended against persistently in current accounting practices. If inventory is valued at the lower of cost or market, why should prepaid insurance not be valued on the same principle? Why should the accountant not inquire as to whether insurance rates have fallen, and if so, take this into consideration in determining the proper amount to carry forward for prepaid insurance? If inventories are carried at the lower of cost or market, why should fixed assets continue to be carried at cost if their market value has decreased? Our present methods of asset valuation are inconsistent in the approach to different types of assets, and this is one of the things that must be corrected.

Many subterfuges have been sought in attempting to avoid some of these difficult problems instead of tackling them. For example, we encounter the suggestion that it is legitimate to distinguish between circulating and fixed capital, or, as it is sometimes put, between current and capital assets. The distinction is intended to differentiate assets purchased for resale from those purchased "to earn income." It is suggested that this justifies valuing the former at current prices and carrying the latter at cost. But this ignores the much more fundamental fact that both types of asset represent expenditures that must be recovered out of revenue ultimately before a figure of net profit can be reached; and that consequently both circulating and capital assets must be carried at current values if a really useful profit determination is to be made.

The only significant difference between current and fixed assets is that the former enter the current year's determination of profit while the latter will be charged against revenue over a longer period. This is an excellent justification of the practice of distinguishing clearly between current and fixed assets in the balance sheet—so as to make the liquid position clear—but not for a basically different approach to "valuation."

The only thing anyone could sensibly mean who says the balance sheet is not a valuation document is that it is not a good valuation document. The task before accountants is to devise ways of making it a more satisfactory valuation document.

Limitations

No matter how well we succeed in improving our techniques, there will inevitably be limitations to what we can achieve. It is not even theoretically conceivable that we could ever produce a valuation document from which an investor could read off a figure and say: "That then is what my shares are worth." The market value of a company depends on a mixture of measurable and unmeasurable factors. For example, if the shares of a company are being bought by a group that is determined to secure a controlling interest, the price of its shares can rise for prolonged periods above what the value of its net assets would suggest. Similarly, the liquidation of a large block of shares can drive the market price down below what might be expected from an analysis of even the best of financial information. These market factors are often quite incalculable. Moreover, some assets are simply not measurable. A particularly skilled executive may be a great asset to a company, but it would be absurd to try to estimate his value to the company in dollars, and to adjust this value up and down as his state of health and peace of mind varied.

We must accept the fact that many important considerations regarding a company cannot be worked out in terms of dollars per share. However, the fact that some factors are not measurable does not absolve us from measuring all the measurable factors as well as we can. Those for whom statements are prepared are entitled to assume that they are the best statements that can be produced; in other words, that the assets that are measurable are included at the best estimate that can be made of what they are worth.

There is no intention here to underestimate difficulties. For example, it is not pretended that it is easy even to decide what assets are measurable and should be included, and what are not. That this is a very tough problem in its own right can be appreciated by running down the assets normally now included in a balance sheet. Cash presents few problems in most cases. With receivables we encounter the problem of collectibility and an element of estimation inevitably enters in. Inventories are more complicated still, and when we get to fixed assets we run into the baffling problems discussed at various times in this text. Goodwill is even more difficult and should perhaps be classified as unmeasurable.

Other financial information

So much attention has been concentrated on the balance sheet and income statement that it might be concluded that it is only in the determination of net income and net worth that valuation is such a decisive requisite. This is not the case: it runs through the whole field of statement analysis.

Consider, for example, the interesting and important calculation of return on investment. This is one of the most popular and useful tools of the statement analyst. Almost everyone who is interested in a company is interested in its return on investment ratio. Does this ratio have any significance whatever if calculated on anything other than the current value of the investment in the company?

Take a simple illustration. Two companies, A and B, are organized at the same date. Each has $1,000,000 invested in it, and each builds a similar plant and starts producing in competition with the other. Let us assume they both provide $50,000 of depreciation a year. Under these ideal conditions for comparison, the return on investment ratio of these companies provides an interesting and valid comparison of their relative efficiency. However, assume a period of prosperity and rising costs (such as we have been going through) and suppose B Company sells its entire plant to C Company for $2,000,000. With orthodox accounting, any possible merit has gone out of a comparison of the return on investment ratio of A Company and C Company. At the same basis of depreciation, C Company will have $100,000 depreciation to provide and will have double the apparent investment of A Company. Yet the two companies will be competing—making the same products in identical plants constructed at the same date. Could this make sense to anyone? Could anyone want or use such figures? This is the basic problem any analyst is up against today and goodness knows what conclusions some of them must be reaching by return-on-investment comparisons.

11

A Program for Accountants

THE CHOICE BEFORE the accounting profession is basically a pretty simple one. They can either accept the proposition that usefulness is the only justification for a set of financial statements, with all this implies, and face up to the problem of producing better statements; or they can attempt to refine their own rules and go on producing statements clearly qualified as to their limitations, in the hope that these may incidentally prove helpful to someone.

It would seem that the profession has actually vacillated between these two approaches. Sometimes we find accountants explaining that financial statements are designed to help the investor value his holdings; and sometimes warning everyone that the balance sheet is not meant to measure value. At the same time, we also hear the importance of consistency being emphasized.

If we are to tackle seriously the problem of producing better statements, this will involve accepting the following propositions:

We must really want to produce better statements—statements that disclose more clearly what is happening. It must be realized that this means management must accept a closer scrutiny of its performance than it gets with the equivocal character of today's statements. It will also mean a much more venturesome attitude on the part of accountants, who must be prepared to become involved in more complicated and difficult valuation problems than they now tackle. Both management and accountants must expect to be exposed to greater risks and criticisms if they accept the wider responsibilities implied—doing so in the confidence that they can defend themselves, if attacked, on the grounds of the reasonableness and skilfulness of their valuations.

The utilitarian nature of financial reporting must be accepted without cavil or quibble. This means that current values have to be adopted as the only legitimate goal of accounting. The obligation to be informative has to be recognized instead of merely the negative goal of avoiding anything that might be misleading.

No satisfactory progress can be expected unless we keep clearly in mind the real nature of the reporting process; that it is essentially a means of communication with the tentative, practical characteristics this implies. It is far closer to a language than to an elaborate philosophical system. To be fully understood, it must be regarded as a means whereby one set of human beings attempts to communicate ideas to another. Improvements will come less from congresses of experts than from the working out of better methods by the practical people whose job it is to prepare published statements.

We must not be too tender on our sacred cows. A great deal of doubtfully valid doctrine has come to be venerated. We must be severe with the High Priests of conservatism, of objectivity, of double entry, and with those who believe that accounting is an end in itself and not a means.

Index